HOT*EXERCISE*

Keep the Burn !!!

Earn the

HOT EXERCISE

HOTWORX®
and the Bold New
Infrared Fitness Frontier

STEPHEN P. SMITH

Printed in the United States of America

Library of Congress Cataloging-in-Publication Data

ISBN#: 978-1-64945-781-3 (PAPERBACK),
978-1-64945-782-0 (EBOOK),
978-1-64945-783-7 (HARDCOVER)
LCCN: 2020910206

This book is dedicated to my daughter, Bria.

Contents

PART III. Getting the Most From Your HOTWORX® Workout

PART IV. HOTWORX® Exercise

PART V. Starting Your Own HOTWORX® Studio

HOT EXERCISE

Introduction

Welcome to the HOTWORX®
Infrared Training System

TIME IS PERHAPS the most valuable commodity we have in life. We might even go as far as to say all human advancement is the result of an effort to improve the quality of time.

Think about it—think about any innovation. Let's take an obvious one, the computer, which was invented to accelerate information processing to make it more readily available. Since its introduction in the 20th century, technologists have endeavored to improve upon the computer's capabilities at an ever-expanding and exponential rate. The Apple Watch or Fitbit you use to accelerate your workout effectiveness is a product of this technology race to satisfy your need to make the most out of every minute of your life. Clothing is yet another example, and the advancement of athletic gear is a category to watch. Think about sweat-wicking material for athletic clothing and companies such as Under Armour. Under Armour exploded into popularity with an innovation that improved body cooling time and utilized compression to promote more efficient blood circulation for faster oxygen utilization to help an athlete gain an edge. Fast food is another example, albeit an unhealthy one mostly, but there are a few good brands, such as Smoothie King and Subway, that are bringing healthy food to you in an expedient and high-quality manner. Healthy delivery companies are paving the way for better, faster food. Muscle

Egg is another innovator of healthy foods. It will deliver super-nutritious egg-white formulation on ice to your front door. Powders are much faster for custom workout hydration now, and HOTWORX® has developed a pre- and post-workout formulation to meet the specific needs of infrared workouts that I will present later in this book.

These innovations are but a few of the many examples of evolution by design that inventors, engineers, and technologists have focused on to improve the quality of time for humans. We want faster delivery, better taste, longer warranties, bigger portions, fewer calories, lower risks, higher returns, and, yes, of course, more workout in less time! The bottom line is most of us want to live longer and have a better quality of life. Goods, services, and experiences that maximize the use of our precious time will always be in demand.

This is so true when it comes to our fitness, and no doubt we are more discerning than ever before in finding the right programs to make the most of our workout time. The four things most of us want to achieve through fitness are to:

- Look better
- Move better
- Feel better
- Live longer

Energy and Heat Accelerate Fitness

The HOTWORX® Infrared Training System, known as 3D Training, is the result of time quality evolution, too. It is the perfect fitness method for the modern world, and it addresses those four things that people demand from their fitness programs. As you will see when you read through the rest of this book, it makes a lot of sense to combine heat and infrared energy with exercise to achieve the most efficient workout possible.

Welcome to the bold new infrared fitness frontier!

Infrared brings another dimension to the fitness table. This is the dimension of energy absorption as a new workout room component. Now people can add components of heat and exercise with infrared energy to the fitness experience for three times the results!

What Is 3D Training?

At HOTWORX®, we have labeled our new workout method 3D Training.

Most people work out in the traditional single dimension of exercise without any environmental considerations. The vast majority of health club workouts take place in an air-conditioned weight room or studio. However, when you add other environmental dimensions to your workout, you force your body to adapt and expose your body to elements that will increase your physical effectiveness.

So, if you could accelerate your results and decrease the amount of time that is necessary for the workout, then wouldn't that be important for both clients and fitness center owners? For the client, it would mean greater results in less time. For the fitness entrepreneur, it would mean happier clients and more facility capacity due to less time that would be needed per workout session. WIN-WIN!

Enter the HOTWORX® 3D Training Method, which involves three components, or dimensions, if you will:

1. Heat
2. Infrared energy
3. Exercise

When these three components are combined into a workout, fitness magic takes place. It's like viewing a film in black and white as it turns into living color. This is why we call it 3D Training.

Dimension 1: Heat

Did you know that when your core body temperature rises, your metabolism speeds up? In fact, for every 1.80°F increase in core temperature, your metabolism speeds up by an incredible 10–13 percent. Not only do you get a better fat burn, but warmups take less time in a heated studio. The warmup that usually takes five to seven minutes takes only three minutes with exposure to the heat. HOTWORX® sauna workouts utilize a temperature level of 125°F.

Champion athletes practice heat acclimation because it has an anabolic effect, which enables them to reach higher levels of conditioning. According to Rhonda Perciavalle Patrick, PhD, increasing your core temperature for short periods may offer dramatic improvements to your athletic performance. She calls this concept "hyperthermic conditioning," which emerging research suggests has multiple positive effects on your body, from increased endurance to the growth of new brain cells.[1] We'll explore hyperthermic conditioning in more depth later in the book.

Dimension 2: Infrared Energy

Infrared is not just an option for creating heat, it is also an energy that, when harnessed properly, has the effect of strengthening and activating the regenerative processes in the human body. Constant exposure to far-infrared radiation, or FIR, can accelerate wound healing and increase collagen content. This helps to explain why workouts in an infrared energy environment can accelerate healing, including workout recovery, along with a host of other beneficial properties, which we'll explore to a greater extent later in this book. For now, it's enough to say that, according to the National Center for Biotechnology Infor-

1. Joseph Mercola, "Are Saunas the Next Big Performance-Enhancing 'Drug'?," Mercola.com, May 24, 2014, http://articles.mercola.com/sites/articles/archive/2014/05/24/sauna-benefits.aspx.

mation, infrared (or thermal radiation) has been used effectively for millennia to treat and/or ease certain health issues.

Infrared energy travels in the form of radiant light waves. After extensive research to understand the proper wavelengths of infrared energy to use for workouts, we determined that exposure to the far-infrared (FIR) portion of the spectrum and a small amount of midrange infrared create the most effective environment for workouts. FIR penetrates more deeply through the skin and produces a very comfortable and more breathable form of heat. Infrared heat is a more natural heat; for example, heat from the sun is infrared. The environment of an infrared sauna has very low humidity and is much more breathable compared with the old-school convection-heater sauna that requires water thrown onto rocks. Better air makes for a higher-quality workout experience.

Dimension 3: Exercise

Two popular forms of exercise work very well inside the HOTWORX® infrared sauna: isometrics and high-intensity interval training (HIIT) and cardio equipment. With isometrics, workouts include yoga, Pilates, and other posture sequenced routines. With HIIT, a 15-minute routine with a cycle or row machine will provide just the right amount of workout results when combined with heat and infrared energy.

By combining the elements of exercise, heat, and infrared energy through the use of our patented sauna for each of the isometric and HIIT workout types, the HOTWORX® 3D Training experience provides an array of time-efficient benefits in every single fitness session.

We'll explore all the benefits of 3D Training in more depth later in the book, but, in a nutshell, working out in a HOTWORX® studio:

- Accelerates your metabolism
- Gets you to your target heart rate sooner
- Forces your body to acclimate to the heat that conditions you for optimum performance in normal everyday environments

Whether you operate a fitness facility or are simply looking for the most efficient way to stay in shape, you can get more done in less time with the HOTWORX® 3D Training Method. This is because when you add heat and infrared energy to your fitness-training regimen, you get the optimum environment. Your workout will yield compounded benefits that stay with you, even if you are forced to take a break from training for some reason. For example, taking a break from training due to injury or for other reasons can often be a cause of major anxiety, so anything that can prolong your fitness level during a forced training hiatus is a good practice to consider.

I know this to be true from personal experience. About 18 months before writing this book, I went in for minor outpatient surgery. I was told by my doctor not to work out for a month following the procedure. When I returned to my workout routine, I picked up where I left off in terms of strength, flexibility, and endurance. I was in the same state of conditioning as I was before the month-long period of not working out. I attribute that to my three years of infrared training before having surgery.

A Booming Industry

When I opened my first gym back in the 1980s, only about 10 percent of the US population was a member of a health club. Since that time, that figure doubled to 20 percent, even as the US population since 1987, when I opened that gym, has increased by more than a third. Back then, the population was 242 million, and today the US population is 329 million. The industry has grown from approximately 24 million health club members to 64 million in that time, an increase of

40 million customers. The population continues to grow, and so does the health club popularity.

It is clear that the industry is very strong and continues to grow worldwide. According to the recent *IHRSA Global Report,* the US health club industry is now valued at more than $30 billion per year. The US leads with the highest number of health clubs at 38,477, with Brazil a close second at 34,509.

As we become more and more health-conscious, and the average life expectancy increases, the demand for fitness options will continue to grow. Of course, 20 percent is better than the 10 percent of the 1980s, but it means we still have some way to go to achieve full fitness participation by the population. The point is that there is plenty of room for industry expansion for many years to come.

Not only has the industry expanded by the number of participants and revenue, but it is also growing by the level of participation as well. What I mean is that people are doing more. Proof of this is that many health club patrons are now members of more than just one club. In many shopping centers and in tightly developed business corridors throughout the country, boutique and specialty fitness clubs are opening everywhere to offer more and more options for the discerning health club goer. It is not uncommon now for a health club customer to hold a CrossFit membership, a multisport and/or large facility membership, and an infrared fitness membership or some other mix of club participation.

A Lifelong Passion

I have been involved in the fitness industry since the age of 18. After my freshman season in college football, I began an intense weight-training regimen for football, and I took on a part-time job at a local gym where I began to sell memberships and to train clients for the owner of the gym. Since that time, I have seen and participated in many different forms of training for football, bodybuilding, and general fitness. I have obtained many certifications, including those in personal training, isometric floor exercise, and TRX suspension training, and have completed many other classes and fitness clinics. After almost four decades observing and practicing many forms of fitness regimes—including weight training, yoga, Pilates, band routines, indoor cycling, and athletic plyometrics—I have come to appreciate workouts that adhere to disciplines involving flow, posture, interval, repetition, and consistency. Discipline to proper form and workout type consistency is of paramount importance to any training routine.

> **I can promise you that the higher the level of workout type integrity, the higher the level of fitness results!**

I remember my very first hot yoga class very well. It was also my first-ever yoga class. I decided to take the class while on vacation during the New Year's holiday in South Beach, Miami. There was a small Bikram studio on the second floor in a location that was tucked away from the ocean and from the busier areas of South Beach. When I arrived at the grungy little studio with my girlfriend at the time, I noticed that there was a space heater plugged into the wall in the front left corner of the room, and the humidity in the room seemed almost unbearable from the very beginning. The air in that dingy and funky little studio was thick and had a vexatious stench.

Nevertheless, we began the session, and even though both of us were in great shape from more traditional fitness programs, we were not in great hot yoga shape! I lasted 20 minutes, and she lasted a little longer, but we both had to exit the studio early. After that humbling experience, I became determined to master hot yoga and not be defeated by my failure with the first class. When I came home from that trip, I began a personal practice of hot yoga, which turned out to be a new beginning for me in fitness.

Since that first hot exercise moment, though, I was hooked by the challenge, and, as an entrepreneur, hooked by the possibilities for a new way of offering heated exercise in a better way and beyond just yoga. "Beyond Hot Yoga" eventually became our first tagline for HOTWORX®. We still use it.

When I was designing the HOTWORX® infrared workout sauna, it quickly became clear in discussions with our manufacturing partner that, to deliver an effective dose of infrared absorption to the human body, participants needed to be exposed to the heat and energy source in a very precise manner. For the proper penetration of infrared waves through the skin, the infrared heat and energy must be dispersed in a way that allows someone to receive the most efficient infrared wave penetration through the skin. This requires using different types of heaters placed in the right areas of the workout environment to spread the infrared heat and energy throughout the space properly for clients. With the use of an EMF testing device, this distribution of infrared radiation can be measured. Through testing with this device, we determined that the subject must be within 1–3ft of the infrared heat source to receive effective energy absorption. The HOTWORX® sauna provides perfect proximity for a small group of people to work out while absorbing a proper amount of infrared.

I discovered the most effective way to deliver an infrared workout was through the use of a sauna built for three people and with exact heater placement, precise ceiling height and wall dimensions with 7x9-ft floor space, and through the practice of very specific flows of workout postures. During an isometric workout session such as yoga, the use of direct infrared heaters and wide-dispersion infrared heaters must be specifically deployed to give the most effective IR exposure. The end result after the development of this infrared workout sauna was the best possible solution for multiple forms of hot exercise.

THE BOTTOM LINE: Infrared precision matters!

The Origin of HOTWORX®

In late July of 2014, I joined a group of friends on vacation to Negril, Jamaica, for five awesome days of sun and cliff-jumping into the beautiful blue waters of western Jamaica. On one of those days, I found myself in a discussion about fitness with Jerome Price, a great friend for the past 27 years and the husband of my longtime business partner Nancy Price, who was on the trip as well. Nancy is a sales expert and has always been in charge of sales for the company. Jerome is a retired high school biology teacher and former competitive bodybuilder, and he holds a master's degree in exercise physiology. I am a certified fitness trainer, former bodybuilder, and arena football player with a master's degree in management. So, needless to say, we found ourselves in deep fitness, business, athletic, and wellness conversations from time to time on that trip. On this particular sun-filled Jamaican day, and after a few rum drinks, we found ourselves in one of those conversations, and it turned to how effective infrared saunas are for workout recovery. We then began to discuss hot yoga. I had been involved in Bikram classes, and I remember talking about the benefits of hot yoga and about the fact that it was great but took too much time for a business executive like me—90 minutes out of my day was just too much. Then, out of nowhere, Jerome said, "People should do yoga in a sauna." For me, that was a eureka moment! Suddenly inspired, I told Jerome, "That is a great idea!" I then told him that when I got back to New Orleans, I was going to design an infrared sauna for isometrics with a small group. In that moment, a fitness invention was born.

When I returned to New Orleans, I did indeed design that sauna. As I described above, I spent hours by myself thinking about the dimensions and placement of infrared heaters and how up to three people could work out inside this new sauna. I remember stepping out the space inside our company war room and performing yoga and other types of isometric postures within what would eventually become a patented design. I filed for a patent in the fall of 2014. After four and a half years and three patent attorneys, the HOTWORX® patent notice of allowance was issued on June 10, 2019.

While the patent is certainly a valuable intellectual property asset, the company name is even more important and perhaps even more valuable. The story of the HOTWORX® name is interesting as well.

At the beginning of what was to become HOTWORX®, the sauna was named Hot Box Detox. That name was cute and somewhat relevant but certainly not a powerful name that could be marketed to the full extent and potential of the innovative sauna. We made an effort to trademark Hot Box Detox to no avail. As it turned out, that roadblock became a blessing. I realized that the only option was to rebrand. Once I made the decision to rebrand, I found myself in the most challenging marketing exercise of my career. I like to tell people that I went through a marketing wormhole to come up with the name HOTWORX®. Many name ideas were considered, ranging from the wild and crazy to the absurd. I eventually decided to hire an online naming portal. So for the fee of $250 to the naming winner and $150 to the portal, I submitted a very precise description of what the name would represent and posted it for a multitude of marketing minds online who submitted naming ideas from all around the world.

I reviewed and scored more than a thousand different name submissions. After hours and hours of analysis and contemplation, I was able to narrow my list to about 20 contenders. I checked all these names for trademark ability with the United States Patent and Trademark Office. I finally chose what I thought was the best submission: HeatWorx. HeatWorx was good but not perfect, plus there were some remote, but potential, trademark issues.

A few days later, I found myself at a CEO roundtable for a half-day conference. There was no way that I could concentrate on the roundtable discussions that day because I was obsessed with finding the perfect name. It was during that conference that it finally dawned on me to replace *heat* with *hot*, and as they say, the rest is history. I checked with the USPTO website and saw that the name was available for a trademark, then immediately emailed and called our legal team to file for the trademark registration of HOTWORX®.

The perfect name had been created, but now we needed a logo for the new brand. I decided to return to the same online naming portal to use their contest format once again to seek a logo design from graphic artists all around the world. The same fees applied—$250 to the winning logo design and $150 to the portal. I revised the name description into a very precise explanation of what was needed for a logo and posted it. I received about 20 logo design submissions, all of which were good but not perfect. Then I received a beautiful work of art from a designer in Indonesia. That submission is the same logo that we now use everywhere for HOTWORX®. We have never changed a thing concerning that original submission. We use the same colors she had used, and we created all our marketing and our 24-hour infrared studio design from that original color palette. During the rebranding process, an article was written about the name change in *Club Solutions* magazine; here is an excerpt:

> The decision to rebrand is never an easy one but is sometimes a necessity. "There was just something missing from the name," said Stephen P. Smith, CEO and Hot Box Detox creator. He went on to explain that the name Hot Box Detox fails to reference the workout done inside of the unit. Yes, you detox with the benefits of infrared heat, but what about the patent-pending fitness program delivering workout sessions through a virtual instructor?
>
> Smith quickly began the exciting journey of rebranding in search of a new name that reflected the true essence of his creation and, of course, has a coolness factor that would resonate with both owners and users. HOTWORX® was a name that embodied all that the brand needed, referring to the workout sessions done inside of the infrared sauna for maximum results.

Together with his executive staff, no time was wasted as the rebranding process was mapped out to ensure a smooth transition from Hot Box Detox to HOTWORX®. As an extra effort, Smith has made the decision to go on a rebranding tour, visiting each location, to personally deliver HOTWORX® marketing materials and replace the door on existing units with a new glass door etched with the HOTWORX® logo.[2]

REBRANDING IN PROGRESS...
VISIT WWW.PLANETBEACH.COM/HOTWORX **FOR MORE INFO**

A Personal Journey

My fitness journey in business began in the fall of 1981 when my college best friend and football teammate persuaded me to join a local gym that had just opened near Southwest Mississippi Community College. This place, the first health club that I had ever been in, was Don's Health and Family Fitness in McComb, Mississippi, the small town where I grew up. Soon after I joined, the owner, Don, told me that I should consider competitive bodybuilding because he thought

2. "'Everything Is in a Name' Says the Owner and Creator of HOTWORX®," *ClubSolutions,* June 8, 2016, https://clubsolutionsmagazine.com/2016/06/hot-box-detox/.

I had potential. A few weeks later, he asked me to work at the gym part-time during the football offseason. I accepted the job and soon learned how to be a trainer for new members and how to make protein smoothies for them to purchase. I was 18 years old. My passion for fitness and the business of fitness had begun.

After obtaining my associate's degree from the community college, I transferred to Ole Miss to pursue my bachelor's. Upon graduating with a degree in political science, I decided to do what you do with a poly-sci degree: I went to grad school. Halfway through my graduate program, my true passion, which was to open a gym, became so overwhelming that I dropped out and opened Bodyplex Fitness Center in my college town of Oxford, Mississippi, in the fall of 1986. I eventually sold that business and opened three Gold's Gym locations, one in Jackson, Mississippi, and two in New Orleans, Louisiana. From there, I went on with my business partner, Nancy, to start a tanning salon franchise—known today as Planet Beach Spray & Spa. Our company still owns and operates that brand along with our rapidly expanding HOTWORX® franchise, which is the first-ever 24-hour infrared fitness studio concept.

I hate to leave any unfinished business on the table though, and I did return to school later in my career to obtain a master's degree in organizational management and to finish a graduate study that I cut short at Ole Miss. It took me a few years off and on, as my work would allow, at night school in New Orleans from a branch of the University of Phoenix, but I did get it done. I am grateful to have gone through that business training as I use it every day in some way.

As time passes, it seems that significant life events come full circle, as they say. Some people like to note that history rhymes with the present, and I would have to agree. A little more than 30 years after opening my first gym, I found myself once again opening a fitness business in Oxford. I chose to include an excerpt from one of my blog articles next to help tell the story of how our version of hot exercise came to be:

So, I'm here in Oxford, MS this week, my second home. This is the town where I attended Ole Miss for my undergraduate degree and where I opened my very first business when I was 23, a basic gym with a weight room and an aerobics studio back in 1986. There were no 24-hour gyms to speak of back in the 1980s.

Fast-forward to 2017.

Once again, in Oxford, I decided to open a gym. This time I had the opportunity to open with three great business partners. My intention was to create a completely new type of fitness facility, one with newly developed, patent-pending, workout conveniences based on heat, infrared energy, and isometrics.

With that goal in mind, the 24-hour infrared fitness studio concept was born.

HOTWORX® became the first-ever fitness studio that enabled clients to experience hot yoga (and over 10 other hot exercise options as well) 24 hours a day, 365 days a year!

When I'm in Oxford (the greatest small town in America, I might add), I spend a lot of time at Uptown Coffee, which is located downtown on The Square, and I often write here. When I first got here today, I sat my computer backpack down in one of my favorite spots and then proceeded to the counter to get some java. When I was checking out, the gentleman behind the counter asked me how long I had been with HOTWORX® (my company affiliation is given away no doubt by the hat I was wearing flipped backward for fitness readiness, lol).

I responded with the story of how we opened the original location here in Oxford on February 13 of last year. It's hard to believe that it has only been one and a half years since that event, but during that time, a lot of life has been lived, and many great workouts have been experienced.

Getting to the point . . . the young barista then went on to ask me about hot yoga, and I told him why he would love our version of hot yoga at 125°F. He also was extremely excited about the HOTWORX® Burn Off App when I told him that it would

allow him to book any workout he wants at any time of day.[3]
Which brings us to the present . . .

The moment you walk into a HOTWORX® infrared workout
sauna, you'll note how you immediately begin to feel good. Your
muscles begin to relax, so you warm up faster, which allows for
better stretching to prepare for the great workout that is about
to ensue. During the workout, you will experience accelerated
sweating and detox. Muscle toning from more heat shock proteins will result in greater strength and flexibility gains. And, of
course, there will be a massive calorie burn!

Simply put, the HOTWORX® workout method provides for a
higher-quality workout with greater results in less time. We believe
it delivers more flexibility, strength/muscle tone, endurance, cardio
conditioning, fat loss, and mind/body detoxification from a single
workout than any other fitness method.

More Workout, Less Time: Why I Wrote This Book

The aim of this book is to help you maximize your workout by sharing
more of the amazing advantages of exercise combined with infrared
energy and heat. I hope to encourage you to consider the advantages
of membership to a 24-hour infrared fitness studio and to provide
you with the research you need in case you'd like to open a franchise
for yourself. Explore with us now as we navigate the bold new infrared fitness frontier!

---

3. Stephen Smith, "The Convenience Factor," HOTWORX® blog, June 25, 2018, https://
hotworx.net/the-convenience-factor/.

PART I

Hot Exercise:
Its History and Benefits

*"The power of heat and energy from light
applied to a workout represents a
bold new frontier in fitness!"*

Chapter 1

The Beginnings of Hot Exercise

FROM THE ANCIENT Roman and Turkish bathhouses to American Indian sweat lodges, many cultures on Earth have a history of sweating practices for mind, body, and spirit. In fact, the practice became so sacred to the Finns they actually used their shared village saunas for bearing children. Throughout history, many indigenous cultures have made use of sweat lodges to cleanse from within and to reach greater self and spiritual understanding.

Thermal medicine, or manipulation of body or tissue temperature for the treatment of disease, can be traced back to the earliest practice of medicine. Cultures from around the world can point to ancient uses of hot therapy for specific medical applications, including cancer. Exercise, too, has been around since ancient times, as the Greeks believed the development of the body was as important as developing the mind. The Greeks held the first Olympics, and the ancient Greek physician Hippocrates, the father of modern medicine, believed that "sport is a preserver of health."

So, historically, when did the combination of exercise with heat begin?

Some scholars trace the origin of hot yoga back to the Hindu Panchgani tapas, a ritual in India known as the "fire sacrifice," which was an ascetic practice to transcend suffering through intentional discomfort. In the modern world of Western sports and fitness, our version of this ritual would probably cause us to proclaim something like, "no pain, no gain," or "work through the pain"!

We do know the first heated workout studio was started by Bikram Choudhury. Born in Calcutta, India, Choudhury started practicing yoga under Bishnu Charan Ghosh. He has said he suffered a knee injury while weightlifting that was serious enough that doctors believed he would never walk again. Given the diagnosis, Bikram developed a practice of traditional yoga poses "in a very specific way, to promote the health and healing of the physical body and mind."[1] Bikram credits this yoga practice of 26 postures and two breathing exercises with healing his knee completely in six months.

Bikram experimented with heat in yoga studios in 1970s Japan, where he noticed that his students exerted themselves more when practicing yoga in the heat. He eventually combined the practice of those postures with a studio heated by space heaters, and thus, hot yoga was born.

When he moved to San Francisco in 1972, he brought the idea of hot yoga to the United States. Bikram eventually became the yoga guru to the stars in Hollywood as his hot yoga business boomed during the 1980s. Recently, Bikram lost a $7 million sexual harassment lawsuit and moved back to India, losing much of his business and his fortune. Aside from the originator's fall from grace, hot yoga has spawned a movement in fitness.

Exercise combined with heat has been popularized by the hot yoga movement for sure, and many hot yoga studios are heated to 104°F by convection heat with a humidity level of 40 percent to re-create the climate of India where yoga originated. Aside from the attempt to give the feel of India in the classes, greater flexibility is the main reason given as to the purpose of heating the yoga studio.

1. Amruta Kulkarni, "The Origin of Hot Yoga," Aura Wellness Center, April 29, 2011, https://www.aurawellnesscenter.com/2011/04/29/the-origin-of-hot-yoga/.

At HOTWORX®, many of the key executives, including me, have taken Bikram and found it to be an excellent practice. However, we have found the air quality to be less than desirable for fitness practice because of the humidity and the convection heat sources. While the humidity may replicate the feel of India, it is not optimal for "hot exercise." Also, because of the "old school" room-heating methods (e.g., traditional central heating, wall or space heaters), the heat is less effective when compared with a true infrared fitness studio. This is why HOTWORX® developed the first-ever fusion of infrared heat and isometrics. HOTWORX® studios, through the use of the patented HOTWORX® saunas, can provide a 30-minute workout at 125°F in clean air with no humidity. The HOTWORX® workouts include a pure isometric workout, including hot yoga, hot Pilates, and other specialty isometric workouts for the core, the butt, and self-myofascial release with foam rollers. In addition to the isometric workouts inside the infrared sauna, HOTWORX® developed and deployed a series of hot HIIT workouts that require only 15 minutes per workout. These HIIT workouts include the use of rowers, indoor cycles, and cycles with upper-body workout levers.

> **Hot exercise can be defined as any workout routine performed within an enclosed workout room or studio that has been heated.**

No doubt, exercising in any heated environment will provide for greater flexibility and sweating during the workout, but those are not the only effects of a properly heated workout environment. Enter the HOTWORX® factor: INFRARED.

Chapter 2

The Infrared Factor

WORKOUTS IN A hot environment created by infrared heaters yield many benefits beyond the typical hot yoga studio environment, including greatly accelerated workout recovery and detox, along with improved metabolic efficiency. Additionally, the air is much more comfortable to breathe during workouts in infrared heat.

Infrared was discovered in the early 1800s by astronomer Sir William Herschel, who noticed radiation when he used a thermometer to measure the temperature of the invisible parts of the light spectrum. Since that discovery, and with the application of electricity, entrepreneurs have been working to monetize infrared. One of the first widespread uses of an infrared application was for heaters that were used to cure the paint of military equipment during World War II. Toward the latter part of the 20th century, infrared saunas began to gain popularity as an alternative to the traditional convection heat saunas for personal therapy and relaxation.

Then, in February 2017, HOTWORX® introduced the first 24-hour infrared fitness studio. The HOTWORX® workouts are shorter because good results can be obtained more quickly with the incorporation of heat and infrared energy into the workouts. The isometric workouts are 30 minutes, and the HIIT workouts are 15 minutes.

Infrared training, for all of its benefits and especially for the
recovery and healing aspects, is becoming another essential
tool for trainers to accelerate results for their clients.

The Science of Infrared

Heat for therapy has come a long way since ancient times, and perhaps the most interesting developments involve something called
"hyperthermic conditioning"—or exercising in the heat. Research
into hyperthermic conditioning is moving forward with the work of
Dr. Rhonda Perciavalle Patrick, a biomedical researcher. Acclimatiz-
ing to heat through the use of hot rooms has been proven to increase
both endurance and the capacity to build muscle. Early evidence suggests hyperthermic conditioning improves the production of human
growth hormone and heat shock proteins—both of which lead to
enhanced muscle growth and healing. As if that weren't enough, Dr.
Patrick argues that it is this acclimatization to heat that produces what
is known as the "runner's high."

As fitness professionals move into the frontier of infrared training, modern hot exercise programs they create should emphasize safe
practice and a "go at your own best pace philosophy." HOTWORX®
uses its patented infrared saunas to promote a safe and effective heated studio with professional virtual trainers who instruct users to stop,
sit, and rest on the mat if any nausea, dizziness, or other adverse feelings are noticed. The virtual instructors, or VIs, as we call them, con-
stantly instruct users to stay hydrated and to work out at an appropriate level of intensity.

How Infrared Works

We know that light travels in waves and that those waves consist of
particles known as "photons." The length of the light wave from crest

to crest determines the color of the light within the visible spectrum, and it determines the effect the light has on objects beyond the visible spectrum as well.

Radiation is generally classified as ionizing or non-ionizing. Ionizing radiation occurs when unstable atoms give off energy to reach a more stable state. Ionizing radiation can alter the basic makeup of DNA and can pose more of a health threat to humans. Much of the health risks with tanning beds, for example, is due to the ionizing rays of parts of the ultraviolet light wavelength.

Somewhere on the UVA to UVB ultraviolet range (to the left of the visible spectrum as depicted in the diagram on the following page), wavelengths begin to generate DNA-damaging light waves. These waves are defined by the dictionary as "high-energy radiation capable of producing ionization in substances through which it passes."[1] It is well known that overexposure to ultraviolet light can cause skin damage and even skin cancer because of the alteration of cell DNA from ionization. The ionizing wavelengths fade out and end within the ultraviolet spectrum as the light waves get longer and begin to fall within the visible.

On the other side, away from the UV radiation (to the right of the visible spectrum as depicted by the diagram), the longer infrared light waves fall just outside the visible spectrum. We know that the wavelength of infrared is non-ionizing and therefore does not damage human DNA. In fact, infrared wavelengths can penetrate the skin up to 1.5 inches or more and can provide many positive benefits to the human body. Some of these benefits include:

- Detoxification
- Improved blood circulation
- Lowered blood pressure

1. Dictionary.com, s.v. "ionizing radiation," accessed May 22, 2020, https://www.dictionary.com/browse/ionizing-radiation.

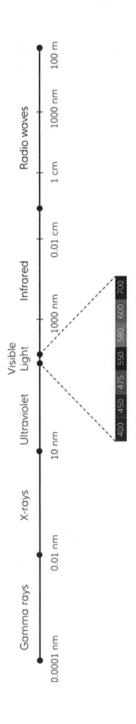

- Suppressed sunburn cell formation
- Treatment for arteriovenous fistula
- Improved sleep
- Reduced pain and stiffness
- Lowered side effects of diabetes
- Improved mood
- Inhibited growth of some types of cancer cells
- Improved motor functions
- Lowered nasal inflammation (allergic rhinitis)
- Increased rate of caloric burn
- Accelerated injury recovery
- Improved immunity functions
- Lowered stress

Concerns over EMF and Infrared Sauna Exposure

There is some confusion today concerning EMF, which stands for the electromagnetic field, and how it relates to infrared saunas and the health effects of these charged particles on the human body. EMFs are electric and magnetic fields of energy that are created by electronic devices, including cell phones, microwave ovens, vacuum cleaners, etc. We, of course, are concerned with infrared sauna heaters, which is also an electrical device that emits low-level electromagnetic radiation.

Electrical currents exist all throughout the natural world, and low-level electromagnetic radiation is generated by the human body through normal chemical reactions.

Though scientifically unfounded, hysteria seems to exist over the issue of EMFs among certain groups of people. Beware of articles you read that fail to cite scientific research! There have been thousands of studies worldwide on the topic of EMFs and public health. The evidence has been analyzed by governmental agencies, and there are no clear connections to an effect on health.

The World Health Organization has this to say about EMFs:

> In the area of biological effects and medical applications of non-ionizing radiation approximately 25,000 articles have been published over the past 30 years. Despite the feeling of some people that more research needs to be done, scientific knowledge in this area is now more extensive than for most chemicals. Based on a recent in-depth review of the scientific literature, the WHO concluded that current evidence does not confirm the existence of any health consequences from exposure to low level electromagnetic fields. However, some gaps in knowledge about biological effects exist and need further research.
>
> It is not disputed that electromagnetic fields above certain levels can trigger biological effects. Experiments with healthy volunteers indicate that short-term exposure at the levels present in the environment or in the home do not cause any apparent detrimental effects. Exposures to higher levels that might be harmful are restricted by national and international guidelines. The current debate is centered on whether long-term low level exposure can evoke biological responses and influence people's well being.[2]

Meanwhile, governmental agencies have consistently concluded based on the evidence that there is little risk of health consequences from exposure to low-level EMFs.

HOTWORX® infrared fitness saunas emit EMF levels that are well within the EPA-recommended exposure levels, which are 0.5–2.5mG, with workouts, performed 1–3ft away from the EMF source and exposure for just 15–30 minutes per workout.

---

2. "What Are Electromagnetic Fields?," World Health Organization (WHO), July 3, 2002, http://www.who.int/peh-emf/about/WhatisEMF/en/index1.html.

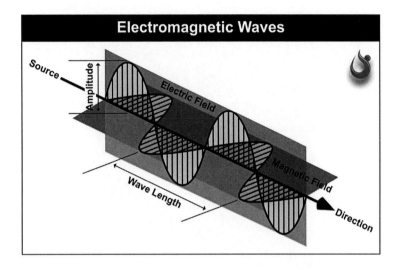

Electromagnetic Field (EMF) as a Measure for Infrared

Infrared is a form of electromagnetic radiation (EMR). EMR, as a current, is surrounded by an electromagnetic field (EMF). For example, lightning is a current between the sky and the ground, or wherever it travels, and an EMF encircles it as it travels. Infrared waves of light energy are surrounded by EMF as well. Therefore, EMF levels can indicate the presence of infrared radiation (IR).

HOTWORX® uses an EMF meter to measure IR presence. Below you will see the level of EMF as measured inside of the workout sauna at 127° Fahrenheit.

Distances of approximately one, two and three feet from the IR source were measured as viewed above in the HOTWORX® IR sauna. As can be seen on the following page, levels of EMF, and therefore IR, can be detected from those distances. Obviously, there is more intensity as you move closer to the heaters. This is why HOTWORX® recommends a workout distance of 1 to 3 feet from the IR source to the human body, so as to maximize the absorption of IR into the skin.

IR is electromagnetic radiation, or EMR.

Let's understand EMR. There are two general types, ionizing and non-ionizing. Ionizing is a more powerful form of radiation and can cause damage to the human body. Ionizing radiation disrupts electrons from their atom orbit and can alter the DNA of cells. By way of example, certain wavelengths of ultra-violet light are ionizing and can cause skin cancer with prolonged skin exposure.

The second type of EMR is non-ionizing. Non-ionizing radiation presents no harm to the human body. It still has the level of energy necessary, though, to move atoms around and cause molecules to vibrate. This process creates heat, but does not displace the orbit of electrons. Infrared is non-ionizing.

Electromagnetic fields are a low frequency and non-ionizing form of radiation. EMF's are created by natural and man-made objects. The sun and even the human body along with electrical devices create IR and, therefore, electromagnetic fields.

As an electrical device, the design of an infrared workout sauna matters, and this is why so much attention was paid to the floor space, and proximity of the client to the IR source for the patented HOTWORX® sauna. Obviously, with the use of an EMF meter, the presence of infrared energy can be detected to let clients know how they are exposed to the beneficial effects of IR absorption while they workout.

Infrared Cellular Therapy

Since the radiant heat from an infrared sauna warms the body from within rather than just heating the body with hot air from the outside, things happen on a cellular level in response to the infrared penetration through the skin.

Here are three responses to this infrared interaction on the cellular level:

1. Breakup of Toxic Substances from Fat Cells

Your body stores toxins and toxicants in fat cells and other fatty organs such as the brain. If fat is absent, you can't store toxins, so keep exercising and eating clean! Furthermore, to take it to a higher level, know that infrared exposure makes the fat-soluble toxic waste removal process from cells more efficient. This is why doctors use infrared sauna therapy to help detox fat cells. (As a matter of reference, it should be noted that toxins originate from natural sources such as poison from a plant or venom from an animal, and toxicants can be natural or from human-made sources such as petroleum exhaust and pesticides. There is a great deal of confusion on what constitutes a toxin. Most people erroneously tend to apply the term toxin to all pollutants.)

Some doctors are now using far-infrared saunas to lower the toxin and toxicant levels within the bodies of their patients. They have discovered that IR sauna temperature ranges of 105–130°F over longer periods of time works well. The lower temperatures help to rid the body of toxic substances stored in fat (a fat sweat). Traditional saunas with higher temperatures produce more of a water sweat.[3]

Specifically, concerning fat-soluble toxins/toxicants, as noted below, research indicates further that detoxing through sweat can be beneficial. Numerous studies have shown that toxic substances including heavy metals, mercury, cadmium, arsenic, lead, and other foreign compounds can be effectively removed from the body through sweat. Sweating can also remove BPA from fat cells. Many experts believe that far-infrared heat, because of its deep penetration through the skin, is most effective for detox.[4]

3. "Infrared Sauna Detoxification," Evolution Health and Fitness, updated 2012, https://www.evolutionhealth.com/sauna-detoxification.

4. Gregg Kirk, "7 Ways to Remove Fat-Soluble Toxins," Ticked Off Foundation, January 28, 2018, https://www.lymeknowledge.com/7-ways-to-remove-fat-soluble-toxins/.

2. Nitric Oxide Effect

For almost two centuries nitroglycerin has been used by doctors to treat heart patients. Nitroglycerin is known to most of us as an explosive. Indeed it was first discovered in the early 1800s and used as an explosive compound. Later in that century, though, it was found to be an effective vasodilator. Nitroglycerin is still used by heart patients to prevent chest pain and heart attacks. Nitroglycerin readily turns into nitric oxide, which is a signaling molecule within the body that helps to increase the width of blood vessels so that more blood can get to the heart.

Nitric oxide can dramatically increase blood circulation. Increased blood circulation has many benefits including that of better organ function and cell growth. Exposure to infrared light can provide the same effect. Exposure to infrared light triggers the body to produce nitric oxide. Within the cells, nitric oxide is generated by arginine and allows the blood vessels to relax, which enables the greater blood flow. Nitric oxide triggered by infrared can relieve pain, lower blood pressure, fight free radicals, and discourage platelet clumping.

The use of infrared saunas and the nitric oxide effect can provide for a noninvasive treatment to improve circulation and avoid trips to the doctor's office!

3. Heat Shock Proteins

Heat shock proteins (HSP) were first discovered in the latter part of the 20th century. Heat shock proteins created from infrared heat exposure can help your body gain strength and retain lean muscle by:

1. Knocking back free radicals (free radicals damage the structure of DNA, which can lead to cancer) to allow for a reduction of catabolism, or the wasting of lean muscle tissue,

2. repairing damaged protein cells, which allows for faster workout recovery, and helping to preserve more of the aminos that are necessary for protein synthesis.

Studies have shown that repetitive visits to the sauna in short 15- or 30-minute sessions for repetitive hyperthermia can result in muscle growth through increased HSPs. More lean muscle is what it takes to achieve improved muscle tone.

Heat shock proteins help to regenerate damaged cells. These proteins are present in all cells, and exposure to infrared heat causes the body to synthesize HSPs. Through renaturation, HSPs gather and recycle damaged proteins. They can also rally the body's T-cells (white blood cells that are important to the immune system) to identify and begin to destroy tumors. A paper published in the journal *Medical Oncology* reports that far infrared can suppress the growth of some cancer cells.[5]

Through HSP and consistent exposure to infrared energy and hyperthermic (heat) conditioning, the rejuvenation of cells can take place. Especially when combined with exercise, this can help to keep the human body toned and rejuvenated.

---

5. "The Effects Inhibiting the Proliferation of Cancer Cells by Far-Infrared Radiation (FIR) Are Controlled by the Basal Expression Level of Heat Shock Protein (HSP) 70A," *Medical Oncology* 25, no. 2 (2008): 229–37, https://www.ncbi.nlm.nih.gov/pubmed/17968683.

Chapter 3

Advocates of Thermal Medicine

ON THE OTHER SIDE OF the fears about exposure to saunas is modern medical research into the benefits of thermal medicine. The research aims to understand the molecular, cellular, and physiological effects of temperature manipulation and the "stress" response, as well as to develop effective and safe equipment for clinical application and temperature monitoring. As a result, today there are a growing number of clinical applications of thermal therapy that benefit patients with a variety of diseases.

Unlike the relatively short history of hot exercise, heat and sweating for therapy has a long history and is well documented as a wellness practice dating back to ancient times. And as the benefits of infrared become more evident and more widely known, the number of doctors using infrared in treatments and who recommend its use also continues to grow. Here follow some examples of how different doctors are actively recommending heat therapy and infrared saunas for all kinds of reasons:

In an online article, bestselling author Joseph M. Mercola, MD recommends heat therapy as a way to increase heat shock proteins to improve blood flow and to rejuvenate the brain. He explains how heat stress can be used to optimize heat shock proteins within your cells, triggering mitochondrial biogenesis. Heat shock proteins promote longevity and assist in preventing muscle atrophy. Dr. Mercola calls the sauna the "poor man's pharmacy" because saunas have proven health benefits, and for the most part, anyone can use them as they become more widely accessible.[1]

Mercola shares that a more frequent sauna regimen of four or more times per week can lead to a reduction in risks of:

- Death from heart disease by 50 percent
- High blood pressure by 47 percent
- Dementia and Alzheimer's disease by 66 percent
- Respiratory diseases and pneumonia by 41 and 37 percent, respectively
- Premature death from all causes by 40 percent[2]

Rhonda Perciavalle Patrick, PhD describes how hyperthermic conditioning by elevating core temperature improves blood flow to all areas of the body through increased plasma volume. She also points out that heat acclimation reduces protein degradation and actually results in net protein synthesis. In her online article, she notes: "You don't need to take exogenous growth hormone. Sauna use can cause a robust release in growth hormone, which varies according to time, temperature, and frequency."[3]

Some research reported in a September 2016 *Time* magazine online article indicates how important regular weekly sauna usage is to

1. Joseph Mercola, "Regular Sauna Use Decreases Disease," Peak Fitness, August 24, 2018, https://fitness.mercola.com/sites/fitness/archive/2018/08/24/regular-sauna-use-decreases-disease.aspx.

2. Mercola, "Regular Sauna Use Decreases Disease."

3. Rhonda Perciavalle Patrick, "Hyperthermic Conditioning," Association for Research on Hyperthermia and Hyperthermic Conditioning (ARHHC), October 17, 2016, http://hyperthermicwellness.com/hyperthermic-conditioning-rhonda-perciavalle-patrick-ph-d/.

health. One long-term study reported that Finnish men who spent two to three days per week in a sauna experienced a 23 percent reduction in risk for heart disease.

Also, the *Time* article quotes Dr. Ernst van der Wall, former chief of cardiology at the Netherlands Leiden University Medical Centre, on the benefits of regular sauna bathing as leading to "a significant increase in heart rate and reduction in total vascular resistance, thereby decreasing blood pressure."[4] In the same article, Dr. Richard Beever, a clinical assistant professor of family medicine at the University of British Columbia, notes that infrared heat penetrates more deeply than just warm air, causing an increased level of sweat.[5]

Brent A. Bauer, MD described for the Mayo Clinic's website that evidence exists supporting the benefits of sauna use for the treatment of chronic illness including high blood pressure, heart failure, dementia, headache, diabetes, and arthritis.[6] According to draxe.com, medical doctor and nutritional practitioner Dr. Lawrence Wilson, who has been using infrared sauna therapy on his patients for more than a decade, reported that "this type of treatment is one of the safest and most useful healing methods he's come across when combined with other factors like a balanced diet."[7]

I'll describe the effectiveness of infrared-induced sweating for detox later in the book, but the evidence continues to mount, as Christiane Northrup, MD, a visionary pioneer and a leading authority in the field of women's health and wellness, writes on her website drnorthrup.com that most sweat is little more than water and salt but

4. Markham Heid, "You Asked: Are Infrared Saunas Healthy?," Time.com, September 7, 2016, http://time.com/4481947/infrared-sauna-benefits-healthy.

5. Heid, "You Asked: Are Infrared Saunas Healthy?"

6. Brent A. Bauer, "What Is an Infrared Sauna? Does It Have Health Benefits?," Mayo Clinic, June 7, 2017, https://www.mayoclinic.org/healthy-lifestyle/consumer-health/expert-answers/infrared-sauna/faq-20057954.

7. Jillian Levy, "Infrared Sauna Treatment: Are the Claims Backed Up?," the official website of Dr. Josh Axe, May 14, 2018, https://draxe.com/infrared-sauna.

notes that studies reveal that up to 20 percent of sweat that is induced by an infrared sauna contains ammonia, cholesterol, fat-soluble toxins, sulfuric acid, and uric acid.[8]

Another advocate, functional medicine expert Alejandro Junger, MD, reminds us that sweating inside heated enclosures has been a part of cultures dating back to ancient Roman, Greek, and Russian civilizations, as well as that of Native American sweat lodges. Sweating has been therapy for people for centuries. Dr. Junger explains how sauna exposure can create a state of self-induced fever, which can condition the immune system for better performance. He points to the fact that skin is our largest organ and is a major toxic waste elimination channel, and through sweating, "one activates and intensifies the elimination of toxins."[9]

Andrew Weil, MD notes through his own personal experience that he is a sauna enthusiast himself. He recommends sauna sessions for cleansing the skin, reduction of soreness, and relaxation. He states that sweat bathing is useful for counteracting overindulgence in drinking and eating as well as benefiting patients who suffer from arthritis, asthma, and respiratory infections and for general body detox to reduce the load of the liver and kidneys.[10]

And, finally, functional medicine expert Dr. Will Cole points to infrared saunas as a "go-to" tool that he recommends to his patients. He is also an avid sauna user to stay on top of his wellness game. He wrote this in his website post about infrared saunas: "Almost every health problem—autoimmune conditions, digestive issues, brain problems, and hormonal imbalances included—can be traced back to inflam-

8. Christiane Northrup, "Infrared Sauna: Can You Really Sweat Out the Toxins?," the official website of Dr. Christiane Northrup, updated June 20, 2017, https://www.drnorthrup.com/infrared-sauna-sweat-toxins/.

9. "The Power of Infrared Saunas," Goop, accessed May 22, 2020, https://goop.com/wellness/detox/the-power-of-infrared-saunas/.

10. Andrew Weil, "Are Infrared Saunas Better?," the official website of Dr. Andrew Weil, May 25, 2017, https://www.drweil.com/health-wellness/balanced-living/healthy-living/are-infrared-saunas-better/.

mation gone wild. Infrared saunas naturally calm down inflammation in the body."[11]

He also cites study results that have shown the benefits of infrared saunas, which include:

- People who suffered from chronic fatigue syndrome saw major improvements after 20 days.
- Infrared sauna use promotes a reduction in the risks related to heart problems and the risk of dying from other health causes.
- People who use saunas four to seven times per week have a 48 percent lower likelihood of dying from heart disease compared with those who used a sauna only once per week.
- BDNF, or brain-derived neurotrophic factor, increases when people practice sauna use and is responsible for creating growth of new brain cells for improved memory and cognitive function.
- Skin hydration and overall complexion improve with increased infrared sauna use.[12]

It is also worth noting that the franchise has been featured twice on hour-long episodes of *The Doctors* TV show. The fact that the HOT-WORX® franchise was invited to be on the show two years in a row is indicative that doctors, in general, are intrigued by the potential for the use of infrared to treat patients, and as a recommended part of individual wellness regimes.[13]

In part II, we'll dive into all these amazing benefits in more depth.

11. Will Cole, "10 Ways Infrared Saunas Take Your Health to the Next Level," the official website of Dr. Will Cole, March 8, 2018, https://drwillcole.com/10-ways-infrared-saunas-take-health-next-level/.

12. Cole, "10 Ways Infrared Saunas Take Your Health to the Next Level."

13. Tim Ferriss, "Are Saunas the Next Big Performance-Enhancing 'Drug'?," the official blog of Tim Ferriss, April 10, 2014, https://tim.blog/2014/04/10/saunas-hyperthermic-conditioning.

PART II

The HOTWORX®
Health Difference

*"Infrared Energy creates a three
dimensional training environment."*

Chapter 4

HOTWORX® for Weight Loss

WHEN YOU COMBINE all the benefits of the far-infrared sauna and all the benefits of exercise, you will experience the HOT-WORX® health difference. Let's begin this chapter with the benefit of weight loss.

Many factors weigh in to determine the rate by which we burn calories, including our age, sex, height, and current weight. There are environmental factors as well, such as air composition and level of temperature. Most people launch a calorie-burn mission to lose fat and drop weight. As a general rule, it takes a 3,500-calorie burn to lose a pound of body weight—which sounds like a lot, doesn't it? But this can be accomplished with just four HOTWORX® sessions because the average person burns 250–450 calories during a 30-minute infrared workout and experiences another 350–600-calorie after-burn during the 60 minutes immediately following the workout.

One of the reasons for this increased calorie burn is that elevating your body's core temperature accelerates your metabolism. In fact, for every 1.8°F your body temperature goes up, your metabolism increases approximately 10–13 percent.[1]

---

1. Erin Coleman, "How Does Body Temperature Affect Metabolism?," FitDay, accessed May 22, 2020, http://www.fitday.com/fitness-articles/nutrition/healthy-eating/how-does-body-temperature-affect-metabolism.html.

Naturally, when training in a heated environment—whether it's running outside in Vegas during the middle of summer or yoga inside of a HOTWORX® infrared sauna—your body's core temperature will elevate more rapidly than when you are working out in an air-conditioned gym or fitness studio. Rapid elevation of your core temperature reduces your warm-up phase and allows you to get to the calorie burn faster. With a heated studio, it takes only a short time with a workout such as Pilates to generate an incredible supercharge to your metabolism/calorie burn. Still, the added bonus is that, as a result, you will also experience the same high-level energy spend during the post-workout calorie after-burn! It's also important to know that through the exercise itself, your body will burn fat because your muscles gain energy from processing fat and sugar that is supplied from your blood.

If your goal through the infrared burn-off process is to lose weight, then I recommend combining your infrared workouts with a daily practice of keeping your body in caloric deficit by eating less than your basal metabolic rate. You can easily calculate your BMR through any number of websites. Just Google around and find one that you like. According to livestrong.com: "When your body is in this state of caloric deficit, it uses your fat stores for energy in a complex chemical process that eventually leads you to excrete most of the excess fat via your lungs." Researchers determined that "the fat actually excretes as about 85 percent carbon dioxide through the lungs and 15 percent water through your urine, feces, sweat, and tears. . . . When you consume more calories than you use, however, your body goes back to filling up the deflated fat cells, and you gain weight."[2]

Here's the punch line.

2. Andrea Boldt, "How Does the Body Excrete Fat?," Livestrong, updated April 23, 2018, https://www.livestrong.com/article/34745-body-excrete-fat/.

For weight and fat loss, our main constituent of body fat,
triglycerides, must be burned up through oxidation.

How It Works: The Infrared After-Burn Effect

Unlike working out in a traditional air-conditioned studio or gym, infrared energy and heat penetrate the skin by 1.5 inches and so, as described above, can accelerate the fat-burning process. Fat breaks down and becomes water-soluble particles at approximately 100.5°F. When fats are broken down into particles, they are more easily flushed by exercise postures, forcing them out of the body through bodily functions, including infrared-induced sweating and through the liver, kidneys, bowels, and lungs.

Infrared exposure, therefore, causes your metabolism to speed up as the waves of energy interact with the cells in your body. This is important, considering that impaired metabolism is associated with obesity. Low-level inflammation is also a contributor to obesity. Compare this fat-burn effect to the melting of candle wax. In the candle-making process, the wax must be heated to its melting point, which is in the 115–120°F range for most types of wax. Fat breaks down as well when your body is heated.

Why Does This Happen?

Exposure to infrared radiation and intense exercise heats up the body. This creates an oxygen deficit. Your body burns calories and oxidizes fat for fuel during and after workouts. The after-burn effect happens during the post-workout period—known as excess post-exercise oxygen consumption (EPOC). EPOC continues until the body reaches homeostasis. This process elevates your metabolism as your body recovers itself back to a pre-workout temperature level. Higher workout intensity levels create longer periods of EPOC. Combining infrared heat with exercise creates higher levels of intensity as the body works to acclimate to the extreme environment.

During EPOC, an increased amount of oxygen is required so that your body returns to its normal rate of metabolism, or homeostasis, following a workout. Most fitness enthusiasts measure the after-burn effect in terms of calories burned within a certain amount of time immediately following the workout. For HOTWORX®, the after-burn is measured during the hour immediately following the workout. It is important to note that EPOC and therefore calories burned within a certain period immediately after a workout vary greatly depending on the intensity of the workout and body composition of the individual.

Calories are interlinked with EPOC. Calories are units of measurement that determine the level of oxygen processed by your body. Oxygen consumption is also the best measure of workout effort. The oxygen consumed by your body is measured by volume—known as VO2, which stands for volume (V) of oxygen (O2). "In essence, VO2 is the best indicator of exercise intensity because it is tied closely to energy expenditure. The higher the intensity, the more oxygen clients consume, and the more calories they burn," Jeffrey Janot, PhD wrote for the IDEA Health & Fitness Association.[3] Adenosine triphosphate, or ATP, is the energy molecules used by your cells. The food that you eat is converted into ATP for use as energy. VO2 determines your body's ability to generate ATP. ATP provides energy to your muscles for your workouts. Your VO2 max, or your maximum level of oxygen consumption capability, is the ultimate factor in determining your cardio fitness level.

The easiest way to measure your body's processing of oxygen is to use a personal fitness tracker. I currently recommend the Apple Watch for reliability and accuracy. Choose a tracker that you trust and find an app that can help you to record and analyze your workout

3. Jeffrey Janot, "Calculating Calorie Expenditure," IDEA Health & Fitness Association, May 31, 2005, http://www.ideafit.com/fitness-library/calculating-caloric-expenditure-0.

intensity levels. You should always inspect what you expect. If you expect to lose weight, then you need to analyze your workout data, mainly calorie burn. If you want to know how intensely you actually worked during your workout, then measure the calories burned during and after.

The more intensity you have with the workout, the higher your level of after-burn.

Of course, working out with infrared heat can really amp up your metabolism and the after-burn effect. Measure the workout after-burn with your Fitbit or Apple Watch following a HOTWORX® session. You will be surprised by how many calories you continue to burn after the workout.

Best Exercise for Max Weight Loss

VO2 max can be improved, and one of the most effective ways to improve it is through HIIT. HIIT, or high-intensity interval training, is a proven training method for elite athletes, enabling them to achieve the highest levels of VO2 max. HIIT can be used by fitness beginners as well, so long as they approach a HIIT workout by going at their own best pace to achieve progress.

In a summary of journal findings, ShapeSense.com notes that "depending on the nature of the training program adopted, someone who is unfit can improve their VO2 max from 5 percent to 30 percent."[4]

Steady-state oxygen consumption aerobics, such as normal treadmill activity, uses the aerobic pathways to produce ATP for storing and using energy.

When ATP is derived from anaerobic pathways, however, the need

---

4. Jordan Daley, "VO2 and VO2max," ShapeSense.com, accessed May 22, 2020, http://www.shapesense.com/fitness-exercise/articles/vo2-and-vo2max.shtml.

for post-workout oxygen is increased and can raise the level of the after-burn, or EPOC effect. Please recognize that this fact can create a false negative set of data when a person is relying on a device that measures calorie burning based primarily on heart rate. Note that the result of a HIIT session might be even more effective than the calorie-burn reading that is displayed on your Apple Watch or your Fitbit might suggest.

Exercise such as HIIT that places a greater demand on the anaerobic energy pathways during the workout can increase the need for oxygen after the workout, thereby enhancing the EPOC. Anaerobic exercise occurs when oxygen demand outpaces the oxygen supply. The EPOC effect is caused by the workout recovery process that includes ATP production, muscle glycogen re-synthesis, blood oxygen restoration, muscle repair with protein, and body temperature restoration. However, if you are looking for a quality EPOC, try HOTWORX® HIIT with the 15-minute Hot Cycle or Hot Row, or HOTWORX®'s latest HIIT workout, Hot Blast, which utilizes the Keiser Total Body Trainer.

There is a way now to benefit from all the advantages of low-impact exercise without sacrificing high-calorie burn or cardio and strength gains. If you want the ultimate 45-minute zero-impact, calorie-scorching workout, my recommendation is a workout such as the HOTWORX® Bonfire, which consists of back-to-back cross-training with different workout types and no break between the workouts. And to prove what an impact it can make on your weight-loss regime, let me share a story of how my lunchtime HOTWORX® team (the team includes myself, and my colleague April Grandbouche and one other coworker at times) does a Bonfire workout on a Monday to kick off the week. The Bonfire workout is a total of 45 minutes of exercise, with 30 minutes of isometrics immediately followed by 15 minutes of HIIT, all done in the infrared sauna at 125°F. The results? I see consistent results with the Bonfire of 600-plus calories burned during the

45-minute ISO + HIIT combo, with another 500-plus torched in the hour after-burn.

Let's put that workout into perspective by looking at the number of calories burned as a ratio to my basal metabolic rate (BMR). BMR represents the total number of calories that your body needs in a 24-hour day to provide energy for your vital functions when you are at rest. The Bonfire 45-minute workout and hour after-burn accounted for nearly 66 percent of my total BMR of 1,675 daily calories (as calculated using Under Armour's MyFitnessPal site).[5] That is approximately 7 percent of my day, generating nearly two-thirds of the calorie burn of my entire BMR! Training hard with a workout like that will get you to a calorie deficit very quickly if you are looking to lose weight and shed fat.

I'll end this chapter with two quotes from the American Council on Exercise:"EPOC is influenced by the intensity, not the duration, of exercise."

"High-intensity interval training (HIIT) is the most effective way to stimulate the EPOC effect."[6]

5. "BMR Calculator," MyFitnessPal, accessed May 22, 2020, http://www.myfitnesspal.com/tools/bmr-calculator.

6. Pete McCall, "7 Things to Know about Excess Post-exercise Oxygen Consumption (EPOC)," the American Council on Exercise, August 28, 2014, https://www.acefitness.org/blog/5008/7-things-to-know-about-excess-post-exercise-oxygen-consumption-epoc.

Chapter 5

HOTWORX® on Energy

WHENEVER I VISIT a new HOTWORX® 24 Hour Infrared Fitness Studio, customers tell me, "I feel so good and so energized when I finish an infrared workout." Of course, finishing any type of workout, infrared or not, makes us feel good and gives a sense of accomplishment, but I have never heard people rave about workouts in the way that they do about the 3D Training Method that combines 1) heat, 2) infrared energy, and 3) exercise.

Why?

Because the effects of infrared training begin the moment the client walks into the sauna and continue throughout the workout and after. The air quality is awesome, and the sweating is accelerated.

The absorption of energy through the skin from the waves of infrared light stimulates cellular activity including nerve cells. Research is beginning to paint a clear picture, as evidence continues to mount, suggesting that infrared treatments can heal wounds, provide cancer therapy and stimulate the brain. This is logical in light of the fact that all life on the planet has evolved for billions of years under the exposure of infrared radiation from the sun. The sun has provided radiation therapy for healing and pain relief since ancient times.

The bottom line is . . .

The human body is very receptive to infrared therapy. This is mainly due to the fact that body composition is primarily made up of water (70 percent), which allows for a very efficient absorption of infrared radiation from sunlight and infrared saunas.[1]

Modern infrared technology has now enabled the creation of workout environments that can provide IR exposure to clients while they work out. We have established that exposure to infrared is stimulating and rejuvenating. When IR is combined with a workout, the effects of working out are then magnified by the infrared.

It makes good sense to elevate the effectiveness of your workout environment and to obtain the highest level of stimulation from your training sessions. One way to do this is to incorporate infrared workouts into your weekly fitness routine.

1. Jordan Daley, "VO2 and VO2max," ShapeSense.com, accessed May 22, 2020, http://www.shapesense.com/fitness-exercise/articles/vo2-and-vo2max.shtml.

Chapter 6

HOTWORX® on the
Immune System

THE IMMUNE SYSTEM is your body's ability to recognize and de- fend itself against infectious bacteria, organisms, viruses, and the development of diseases. The lymph system consists of tissues that store white blood cells that are used for fighting disease within the body. The lymph nodes are the radar for the body, providing early de- tection when harmful organisms have made their intrusions into the body. Upon detection, the lymph system is prompted to make more infection-fighting white blood cells called lymphocytes.

Far-infrared (FIR) exposure provides a natural way to enhance the human immune system.

"Far-infrared saunas provide an incredibly gentle, side-effect-free, effective mechanism for detoxification for all of my patients, even the sensitive ones," Rachel West, MD told *Massage* magazine.[1] Through

---

1. Jonny Bowden, "Far-Infrared Saunas and Lymphatic Massage: A Healing Combina- tion," *Massage*, May 31, 2013, https://www.massagemag.com/far-infrared-saunas-and-lym- phatic-massage-a-healing-combination-12683/.

the heating of the core body temperature and through the penetration of infrared energy, far infrared (FIR) raises the body's core temperature, creating an artificial fever that boosts your immune system. A fever fights against disease by neutralizing bacteria and virus infections. A FIR-induced fever increases the count of white blood cells and killer T-cells. T-cells kill cancer cells and other cells that are infected with viruses along with cells that are otherwise damaged and need to be eradicated from the body.

It is well documented that sweat induced from FIR is much better for detox. Studies show that there is up to seven times more toxic substances, fat, and impurities in infrared sweat than sweat from traditional heated environments. The body functions more efficiently in a clean, detoxified state.

Exercise can also assist in building your immune system. There is a commonly held belief that people who practice yoga are far less susceptible to colds in the winter due to their boosted ability to fight off germs that cause sickness. Yoga can help to regulate your immune system as it relieves stress. Most yoga postures, especially forward bends, such as a downward dog, can provide a calming effect to the body.[2]

Imagine how beneficial your workouts could be if you combined yoga with infrared sauna therapy!

---

2. Timothy Burgin, "Yoga Therapy for Colds and Flu," YogaBasics, accessed May 22, 2020, https://www.yogabasics.com/learn/yoga-therapy-for-colds-and-flu/.

Chapter 7

HOTWORX® for Youthful Skin

LET'S FACE IT. Our skin takes a beating everywhere we go. Every day, because of environmental factors, including such things as exposure to UV and air pollution, our skin is under assault. To counter this, why not treat your skin each time that you work out, while you are working out? As the old saying goes, kill two birds with one stone—or a more modern way to say it, let's multitask. Give your skin rejuvenation while you derive all the mental and physical benefits of a great workout!

I hear from our customers all the time about how much better their skin looks and feels after a workout in the infrared sauna, and you might ask, Why would this be the case after a far-infrared (FIR) exercise session? Let's take a look at the science. I stumbled across a government website called PubMed Central, a repository of journal literature run by the National Library of Medicine. The website had republished an abstract from this study: "Effects of Infrared Radiation on Skin Photo-Aging and Pigmentation," which was published in 2006.[1] The study set out to determine the effects of infrared radia-

---

1. Ju Hee Lee, Mi Ryung Roh, and Kwang Hoon Lee, "Effects of Infrared Radiation on Skin Photo-Aging and Pigmentation," *Yonsei Medical Journal* 47, no. 4 (August 31, 2006): 485–90, https://doi.org/10.3349/ymj.2006.47.4.485.

tion on the production of elastin and collagen. Twenty female patients who had mild facial wrinkles and pigmented lesions were treated with daily exposures of FIR radiation for six months.

> The study found that the amount of collagen and elastin increased in proportion to the duration of FIR treatments. After six months all participants had a 51–75 percent improvement in roughness and texture of the skin, as well as a 25–50 percent improvement in color and tone of the skin.[2]

This study showed that IR exposure is an effective, nonablative (nonabrasive, no skin peeling) way to rebuild collagen and elastin, and to treat the effects of photoaging! The abstract goes on to note that several studies have shown that FIR exposure can also accelerate the healing of wounds because of this collagen increase and the stepped-up process of cell production.

So, go ahead, multitask, and get more from your workout in less time by rejuvenating your skin while you train!

---

2. Lee, Roh, and Lee, "Effects of Infrared Radiation on Skin Photo-Aging and Pigmentation."

Chapter 8

HOTWORX® for Detoxing

SHERRY ROGERS, MD, author of *Detoxify or Die*, has this to say about toxic substances and detox:

"Studies now confirm that diet and environmental chemicals cause 95% of cancers. Since the far-infrared sauna is the safest, most efficacious, and economical way of depurating stored toxins, this makes it a household necessity."[1]

I remember seeing a newsfeed declaring, "1 in 6 deaths on the planet are linked to pollution." My first thought was, How shocking, and my second was just sadness. We are destroying our environment and killing ourselves in the process. When I searched to find that news story, I discovered the *Lancet* Commission on pollution and health. From the *Lancet* Commission report, I learned that pollution causes more disease and premature deaths than any other thing in the world today, including 9 million premature deaths in 2015, a full 16 percent of all deaths for that year! This was three times more than from AIDS, tuberculosis, and malaria and 15 times more than all forms of violence including wars.[2]

---

1. Sherry Rogers, *Detoxify or Die* (Sarasota, FL: Sand Key Company), 2002.
2. Philip J. Landrigan, Richard Fuller, Nereus J. R. Acosta, Olusoji Adeyi, Robert Arnold, Niladri (Nil) Basu, et al., "The *Lancet* Commission on Pollution and Health," *Lancet* 391, no. 10119 (February 3, 2018): 462–512, https://doi.org/10.1016/S0140-6736(17)32345-0.

Modern pollution is created from chemicals, exhausts, and fumes as opposed to the traditional wood-burning stoves, fireplaces, and dirty water, and it is on the rise. For the big picture, we should all try to do our part to save the planet, such as paying attention to how we handle our waste and how we source our energy needs. On a very personal level, though, we should learn how to manage the pollution that we absorb, and encourage our friends and family to do the same if we want to live longer and have a better quality of life.

But the point is that every day we are victims of assault! Our bodies are attacked by air pollution, processed foods and drinks, and toxins and toxicants that we touch and are absorbed into our skin. As the toxicity of our environments continues to increase, now more than ever, we need a strategy for personal detoxification. One way to counter the daily assault on our bodies is to practice detox through infrared heat. Inside an infrared sauna, the energy and heat penetrate the body very deeply, and, in doing so, it stimulates detoxification at the cellular level. Check out the following segments to gain a better understanding of how exposure to infrared energy can help with your detoxification needs.

Sweat It Out

In the Ayurveda/yoga world, the Sanskrit word for *sweat* is one of five curative therapies known as *panchakarma*. Beyond sweating, there is also the body responses to heat that include increased white blood cell production, relaxation, improved immune system, and an increased level of healing of connective tissues.

Ayurveda, developed in India more than 3,000 years ago, is an ancient form of holistic healing practiced as a method that requires the balance of the mind, body, and spirit. In the language of ancient India, Sanskrit, Ayurveda means the "science of life." Historians believe Ayurveda to be one of the oldest healing sciences. Ayurveda and yoga are considered sister practices. The literal meaning of yoga in Sanskrit is "yoke," which denotes a union of body and spirit.

As your body responds to hot yoga, it strengthens, detoxifies, and heals. Sweating from hot yoga, and all other forms of hot exercise, provide for even more detoxification. Specific to sweating, there is mounting scientific evidence to indicate that it can take a lot of stress off your kidneys and colon when it comes to the body's need to rid itself of toxic waste.

The skin is the body's largest organ, and it can play a larger role in detox if you use it to do so. The level of toxicity present in your body is relative to how efficiently your body can rid itself of these impurities, so why not use your skin to its maximum detox potential? Sweat rids the body of dangerous water-soluble toxicants, such as heavy metals, and oil-soluble toxicants such as gasoline and pesticides.

In Mark Sircus's book *Far-Infrared and Vibrational Medicine*, he explains that treatment for heavy metal toxicity is complex. He explains how the skin is one of the most overlooked pathways to body detoxification. The skin can provide for one of the most effective means of detoxification through the process of sweating.[3]

The skin accounts for approximately 7 percent of body weight and acts as a border exchange between elements outside and within the body. If manipulated properly, the workout environment can greatly enhance the body's ability to enable the exit of toxic substances through the skin using sweat as the transportation medium. Toxins and toxicants that exit through the skin are more easily controlled than that of the internal organs. Twisting postures that accelerate circulation combined with deep penetrating infrared energy and heat can greatly enhance this process during workouts.

In his book, Dr. Sircus notes how important sweat therapy can be when it is used to rid a patient of toxicity by describing one of the

3. Mark Sircus, *Far-Infrared and Vibrational Medicine* (self-pub., Amazon.com Services LLC, 2015), Kindle.

worst cases of environmental toxicity in US history. He shows how Dr. Grace Ziem used the treatment. Dr. Ziem utilized sauna therapy on his patient to the point where the toxic substances could be clearly seen on the towels used to wipe the patient's sweat.

Additionally, Sircus's book quotes Dr. Dietrich Klinghart, a frequent infrared sauna user himself. He makes a clear point that "far infrared saunas can mobilize mercury in deeper tissues." He makes a strong case for the use of infrared sweating to bypass, or take a load off, the kidneys and large intestines for toxic substance elimination.

As he makes that case, he notes how the use of infrared saunas accelerates vital organ and gland metabolism, neutralizes bacteria, molds, fungi, and yeasts, and promotes exercise of the heart. He also talks about the use of IR saunas for lowering of blood pressure and dilation of blood vessels, resulting in pain relief, accelerated healing, and relaxation.[4]

Sweat it out to provide relief to your internal organs for detox, and remember that infrared sweating provides for a much greater level of detoxification. Add even more detox when infrared heat and energy is combined with exercise.

Compression for Detox

Of course, it is easy to equate sweating with detoxification. What is not so easily understood is detoxification based on muscle compression. When you flex your biceps doing curls, you are compressing your muscles and constricting blood flow. When you relax the flexion, you can feel the flush of the constricted blood flow as it releases. When this happens, toxic substances are flushed more rapidly through and eventually out of the body.

The constant compression holding and releasing during an isomet-

---

4. Sircus, *Far-Infrared and Vibrational Medicine.*

ric workout is an excellent way to detoxify the body. When this iso-metric muscle compression is combined with infrared heat, the detox process is supercharged!

Yoga uses isometrics in a sequence and places emphasis on breathing to further promote detox. The HOTWORX® series of isometric and HIIT workouts utilize a specially designed far-infrared sauna to provide for the execution of a fitness and detox strategy within the same training session. I would recommend at least three infrared workouts per week for general fitness and detox.

What is more, far-infrared sweating is superior to traditional sauna sweating because FIR saunas generate more sweat at lower temperatures (for HOTWORX®, the ideal workout temperature is 125°F). In contrast, conventional saunas require 180°F to more than 200°F to get similar sweating volume results. It is worth mentioning again that sweat from an infrared sauna has been proven to contain five to seven times more toxic waste than that of a traditional sauna.

Take a load off your internal organs. Sweat it out. Nothing makes you feel more refreshed than a good sweat from a great infrared workout. The more you sweat, the more you detox your body.

Chapter 9

HOTWORX® on Mental Function

WHAT COULD BE MORE important than our brain health? Of course, any form of exercise is good for stress relief and cognition. Therefore, as fitness advocates, trainers, and fitness club owners, we should go beyond the biceps and begin to focus on exercise that is better for the brain.

Developing good habits to improve thinking, understanding, learning, and memory recall is obviously important, and fitness programs should place more emphasis on them. To that point, workouts combined with exposure to infrared heat can be a powerful exercise for the brain!

Cardio exercise can kick-start the level of brain-derived neurotrophic factor (BDNF) by launching the creation of new brain cells as well as neural pathways and connections. Working out also increases neurogenesis for the formation of new neurons, and enhances blood flow and oxygen transport for improved cognitive functions.[1]

Now, let's think about combining infrared energy and heat with a workout. It has been shown that infrared sauna exposure and the high

1. Carrie Myers, "Creating the Ultimate Mind-Body Connection," the American Council on Exercise, October 2011, https://www.acefitness.org/certifiednewsarticle/1748/creating-the-ultimate-mind-body-connection/.

cardio effects of HIIT training both increase the levels of brain-derived neurotrophic factor (BDNF). A combination of the two can be even more effective.

Infrared Energy + Heat + Workouts = Brain Power

What you should do now is to try one of the HOTWORX® HIIT or isometric infrared workouts. You will notice immediate mood upswings beyond the effects of normal workouts in an air-conditioned gym.

Consider the following infrared research from the Department of Psychology and Institute for Neuroscience at the University of Texas–Austin:

> Researchers compiled data to imply that transcranial, or through the skull, infrared laser stimulation may be an effective and noninvasive way to improve the functions of the brain with respect to cognition and emotions. This transcranial approach has proven to be safe for treatment of strokes. Researchers concluded that this could lead to future development of performance enhancement through noninvasive methods for brain rehabilitation.[2]

I can personally attest to the immediate boost to mental clarity that one infrared workout can provide. I always notice an instant increase in mental focus when I begin to do work for my job right after a HOTWORX® session. The improved circulation and boost of oxygen to the brain could be one reason for this effect.

---

2. DW Barrett and F. Lima-Gonzalez, "Transcranial Infrared Laser Stimulation Produces Beneficial Cognitive and Emotional Effects in Humans," *Neuroscience* 230 (January 29, 2013): 13–23, https://www.ncbi.nlm.nih.gov/pubmed/23200785.

What About Other Benefits to the Brain?

Researchgate.net reported in November 2012 a study in rats and another in humans involving the use of infrared lasers to modulate mood and to alleviate depression. The report also suggested that neurological conditions related to compromised neural metabolism might be treated with an infrared performance-enhancing intervention. The same researchers published another paper two years later reporting that transcranial infrared stimulation may be effective for mitochondrial respiration in neurons.[3]

Let me put it into layman terms. You have more than likely been to the beach and have felt the warmth of the sun on your body. The mental rejuvenating effects of a trip to the beach is undeniable. Of course, the warmth that is felt from the sun at the beach is infrared energy penetrating the skin.

The infrared energy may penetrate deep into the body, possibly including the brain through openings around the eyes, during a HOT-WORX® sauna workout, too. Without a doubt, better circulation can be obtained from an infrared workout, meaning more blood flow and oxygen transport to the brain. It is quite possible that combining the elements of infrared energy and heat with your workout can give you better "brain" results than what you can obtain in a traditional gym environment.

Dual Benefits

Just as exercise is good for the brain, so is infrared heat. Therefore, it makes sense to benefit from both at the same time.

A 2013 *Huffington Post* article asserts that 20 minutes of yoga is

3. F. Gonzalez-Lima and Douglas W. Barrett, "Augmentation of Cognitive Brain Functions with Transcranial Lasers," *Frontiers in Systems Neuroscience* 8, no. 36 (2014), https://www.ncbi.nlm.nih.gov/pmc/articles/PMC3953713/.

good for the brain. The article published on huffingtonpost.com cites a study published in the *Journal of Physical Activity and Health* that included 30 female college students who performed 20 minutes of yoga and 20 minutes of exercise on a treadmill. Participants in the study took cognitive tests after the yoga session and again after the treadmill session. Results showed higher scores for tests following the yoga sessions.[4]

Isometric exercise, combined with infrared, which places emphasis on proper breathing and the connection of physical performance and mental awareness, may produce similar brain-enhancing results. HOTWORX® provides multiple hot isometric routines that guide you through mind-breath-body workouts for heightened mental awareness.

HOTWORX® provides many exercise routines to choose from, all created for use inside an infrared sauna at 125°F. The combination of the infrared energy, the heat, and the exercise routines provide for multi-dimensional workouts that are good for the brain.

---

4. "What 20 Minutes of Yoga Does for Your Brain," *Huffington Post*, updated June 11, 2013, https://www.huffingtonpost.com/2013/06/10/20-minutes-yoga-brain_n_3404766.html.

Chapter 10

HOTWORX® on Your Mood and Emotions

TAKING CARE OF YOURSELF could quite possibly be the greatest gift that you could give to your loved ones. Why? Because when you feel good about yourself, then you treat others even better. There is research to support this idea. One sure way to feel better about yourself is to go work out.

Working out delivers a guaranteed mood swing to the positive. Stress seems to evaporate during and after a great workout. Infrared light also promotes a good mood through the production of serotonin. Higher levels of serotonin help to improve your mood. Serotonin is a chemical found in the human body, a neurotransmitter that carries signals alongside the nerves.

Serotonin is thought to be especially active in constricting smooth muscles, transmitting impulses between nerve cells, regulating cyclic body processes, and contributing to well-being and happiness.[1] Most research agrees that serotonin is responsible for mood balance. Higher levels of serotonin lead to better moods, and a deficit in serotonin

---

1. James McIntosh, "What Is Serotonin and What Does It Do?," Medical News Today, February 2, 2018, https://www.medicalnewstoday.com/articles/232248.

can lead to depression. Infrared light, exercise, and diet are proven ways to increase levels of serotonin. Exposure to infrared can produce immediate positive mood swings. When you walk into an infrared sauna, the effects are felt immediately.

Science supports this, as shown by research conducted at the University of Wisconsin-Madison. Clear improvement in patients suffering from depression was documented when they were exposed to energy and heat from infrared lamps.[2] Remember my earlier point about the mood-uplifting effect of sunlight at the beach? Simply put, infrared makes you feel good!

According to a recent article in WebMD written by Charles Raison, MD, two new studies using an infrared heating device on individuals with depression have shown positive outcomes for depressive symptoms. Raison reports that a single hyperthermia (infrared heat) treatment reduced depression scores by more than 50 percent in 16 individuals who were tested, and this was five days after the treatment![3]

Hot yoga and other hot workout forms are gaining tremendous popularity and for a good reason. One of those reasons is the positive effect on a client's mood during those workouts. Workouts, in general, are good for your mood, and hot workouts are even better . . . but when infrared is added to the equation, your mood and sense of well-being are elevated even more.

Defeat SAD with Infrared

Seasonal affective disorder, known by its acronym SAD, is a form of depression due to light deprivation. This type of depression happens

2. Relaxnews, "Infrared Heat Eases Depression Symptoms, Study Finds," CTV News, May 17, 2016, http://www.ctvnews.ca/health/infrared-heat-eases-depression-symptoms-study-finds-1.2905272.

3. Charles Raison, "Can Sitting in a Sauna Ease Depression?," *WebMD Blogs*, July 7, 2016, https://blogs.webmd.com/mental-health/20160707/can-sitting-in-a-sauna-ease-depression.

during the fall and winter months when there is less available sunlight. The symptoms cause your energy levels to fall to lower levels and affect your mood, causing feelings of depression. Light therapy has proved to counter the symptoms and improve mood. Infrared is one form of light therapy and is an effective way to treat the symptoms of SAD.

Two important studies support the use of infrared as a treatment for SAD. In the first study, there were three groups. One group received bright light treatment, one group received infrared light, and one control group received no treatment. Both the bright-light group and the infrared group were more effective than the control group, and the infrared group was just as effective as the bright light group.[4]

In the second study, it was noted that light therapy was less effective in treating SAD than summer sunlight. Of course, we know that sunlight delivers infrared to an individual in addition to the visible light spectrum. In this study, 17 mice were used with one exposure group of eight mice who received infrared for 60 minutes per day over four weeks. The results showed that the exposure group reached a statistically significant level of difference, confirming the potential for the use of infrared radiation for mood treatments based on the antidepressant effects that were observed.[5]

I hear all the time from franchisees, and read reviews from customers of HOTWORX®, with the same post-workout comment: "I feel so good after a workout in the infrared." Infrared has a very uplifting effect on your mood and now has been shown through scientific research to be a positive treatment for SAD.

4. Ybe Meesters, Domien G. M. Beersma, Antoinette L. Bouhuys, and Rutger H. van den Hoofdakker, "Prophylactic Treatment of Seasonal Affective Disorder (SAD) by Using Light Visors: Bright White or Infrared Light?," *Biological Psychiatry* 46, no. 2 (August 1999): 239–46, https://www.researchgate.net/publication/12880246_Prophylactic_treatment_of_seasonal_affective_disorder_SAD_by_using_light_visors_Bright_white_or_infrared_light.

5. Jui-Feng Tsai, Sigmund Hsiao, and Sin-Yao Wang, "Infrared Irradiation Has Potential Antidepressant Effect," *Progress in Neuro-Psychopharmacology and Biological Psychiatry* 31, no. 7 (November 2007): 1397–400, https://www.researchgate.net/publication/6219980_Infrared_irradiation_has_potential_antidepressant_effect.

Chapter 11

HOTWORX® on Sleep

THERE IS A SYMBIOTIC RELATIONSHIP between working out and sleeping. For better workouts, you need better sleep. For better sleep, you need better workouts. So go the yin and yang of life in fitness. It stands to reason that we should seek the very best workouts we can find. These workouts should yield better physical (and mental) results in less time—in other words, a more evolved level of quality. That being said, you can increase your workout quality by adding more heat and energy to your workout environment (we call this HOTWORX® 3D Training) if you are seeking to improve sleep and reduce stress.

Let's take a look at some of the science.

Dr. Michael Hamblin, a Harvard professor, has published close to 300 papers, many on phototherapy. In an interview with *SelfHacked*, discussing why some people get tired after low-level laser therapy, he said that "light therapy somehow releases the block that stops them from sleeping, by perhaps relaxing them." The article goes on to report how light therapy lowers glutamate, which reduces overexcitement in the brain. That serotonin metabolism is positively affected as there are more serotonin metabolites in the urine when people are exposed to infrared.[1]

---

1. Joe Cohen, "Dr. Michael Hamblin Interview: Infrared Therapy Expert," *SelfHacked*,

From my experience, I know I get higher-quality sleep when I am on a weekly workout schedule that includes three to four HOT-WORX® training sessions. I also know from personal experience that my sleep is not as good when my weekly workouts do not include infrared. The daily fitness goal needs to include seven to eight hours of sleep and scheduled time for exercise, including infrared, to find the right balance. Since we know the body recovers from workouts more efficiently with sufficient, quality sleep, then why not add an element to your workout environment that is backed by science as a way to improve your sleep, such as infrared?

If you have ever experienced poor sleep quality, then you know it can be detrimental to your work productivity and to your general quality of life. Simply put, you feel like crap when you don't get enough sleep. I experienced poor sleep until I discovered infrared sauna workouts. For the past three years, my sleep has been greatly improved with regular infrared workouts. Unfortunately, not a lot of research exists on the link between better sleep and exposure to infrared. But we do know that sleep deprivation causes the buildup of free radicals in the brain that can cause damage over time, and we know that infrared stimulates antioxidants that may counteract free radicals. Nevertheless, it's obvious how much better we all feel during the day following a great night of sleep.

The goal is to achieve slow-wave sleep, or deep sleep, on a regular nightly basis.

Webster's defines slow-wave sleep as a state of deep, usually dreamless sleep that is characterized by increased delta waves and a low level of autonomic physiological activity.[2] It is hypothesized that saunas

---

updated March 23, 2020, https://www.selfhacked.com/blog/interview-with-dr-michael-hamblin-harvard-professor-and-infrared-therapy-expert.

2. *Merriam-Webster*, s.v. "slow-wave sleep," accessed May 22, 2020, https://www.merriam-webster.com/dictionary/slow-wave%20sleep.

condition the body and the brain for deep sleep by heating the body, and through the cooling process, better sleep is induced. It has been established through research that regular weekly exercise can increase slow-wave sleep as well. Therefore, it is certainly possible that combining infrared with working out may have a positive effect on sleep.

Quoting from Psychologytoday.com: "A recent National Sleep Foundation poll found that regular exercisers were significantly more likely to report sleeping well on most nights than people who were not physically active."[3] Research tells us that the amount of quality sleep is enhanced by exercise, but common sense should dictate that to us, as well, the fact that consistent workouts are great for sleep.

In a sleep study involving heat, an infrared sauna was used to determine how effective it was for patients who suffered from chronic fatigue syndrome (CFS). As of the date of the study, there was no definitive therapy for CFS. Ten inpatients were observed. Perceived fatigue was significantly decreased following infrared sauna therapy. Negative mood, anxiety, depression, and fatigue were significantly improved. No patients reported any negative effects from the infrared therapy. The study concluded that thermal infrared sauna therapy may be a useful and safe treatment for chronic fatigue syndrome.[4]

In another study, exercise was tested to see if a structured program of physical fitness activities could reduce insomnia. The study concluded that aerobic physical activity is an effective treatment "to improve sleep quality, mood, and quality of life in older adults with chronic insomnia."[5]

3. Michael J. Breus, "Better Sleep Found by Exercising on a Regular Basis," *Psychology Today* (blog), posted September 6, 2013, https://www.psychologytoday.com/hk/blog/sleep-newzzz/201309/better-sleep-found-exercising-regular-basis-0.

4. Y. Soejima, T. Munemoto, A. Masuda, Y. Uwatoko, M. Miyata, and C. Tei, "Effects of Waon Therapy on Chronic Fatigue Syndrome: A Pilot Study," *Internal Medicine* 54, no. 3 (2015): 333–38, https://www.ncbi.nlm.nih.gov/pubmed/25748743.

5. Kathryn J. Reid, Kelly Glazer Baron, Brandon Lu, Erik Naylor, Lisa Wolfe, and Phyllis C. Zee, "Aerobic Exercise Improves Self-Reported Sleep and Quality of Life in Older Adults with Insomnia," *Sleep Medicine* 11, no. 9 (October 2010): 934–40, https://www.ncbi.nlm.nih.gov/pmc/articles/PMC2992829.

Lack of a large body of research on the topic aside, I can tell you from my own personal experience that regular workouts involving detoxification through sweating can be great for sleep. Furthermore, I know that I can accomplish this through exercise combined with infrared energy and heat.

Chapter 12

HOTWORX® on Hyperthermic Conditioning

HYPERTHERMIC CONDITIONING is a fancy way to describe the positive thing that happens to your body when you acclimate it to heat while working out in a heated environment such as a HOT-WORX® sauna. Working out has its obvious benefits, but when combined with heat, wonderful fitness advantages begin to happen as your body adapts to the heat!

As your body acclimates to the heat, plasma volume and blood flow to your heart and muscles increases, resulting in higher levels of athletic endurance. This also causes an increase in muscle mass from accelerated production of heat shock proteins and growth hormone.

According to Dr. Rhonda Perciavalle Patrick, who originated the term "hyperthermic conditioning," two 15-minute sauna sessions separated by a 30-minute cooling period may boost your HGH by fivefold. I encourage you to read up on her work. In her article, Dr. Patrick summarizes one point by highlighting three areas of benefit from acclimating the body to heat stress ("hyperthermic conditioning") via a sauna. These areas include enhanced endurance, increased muscle gains through a massive release of growth hormone, and greatly improved brain function. She comments brilliantly, as she begins to summarize, with the fact that increased stress to the body through working out "somewhat paradoxically" causes the body "to become more resilient to stress through stress itself."[1]

The bottom line is . . .

Add hyperthermic conditioning to your athletic training or general fitness routine. HOTWORX® can provide the hyperthermic conditioning that you need with infrared sauna hot exercise for accelerated training results.

Another way to promote lean muscle growth is through improved workout recovery from infrared sauna exposure. It's no secret that infrared heat is also good for healing overworked muscles.

1. Joseph Mercola, "Are Saunas the Next Big Performance-Enhancing 'Drug'?," LewRockwell.com, May 26, 2014, https://www.lewrockwell.com/2014/05/joseph-mercola/promote-muscle-growth-longevity-new-brain-cells/.

Chapter 13

HOTWORX® on Productivity

THE FACTS SUPPORTING the belief that fitness improves productivity are overwhelming. Study after study proves commitment to exercise will boost your alertness, help prevent illness, improve your mental health, and make you more disciplined. All of these things together will make you a work machine! And there is nothing more satisfying than achieving career success and receiving praise from your peers for a job well done.

It's worth noting that alertness is one of the most important traits for work productivity. Alertness leads to improved focus, and there is nothing better than a morning workout or lunchtime fitness routine to boost your workplace focus. My weekly routine consists of weight training each workday morning followed by a 30-minute lunchtime HOTWORX® isometric session. I feel energized throughout my entire workday when I'm fueled by great workouts. Alertness happens through workouts when more oxygen is supplied to the brain, so give your work brain a workout boost!

I believe in small-group training, and I am a member of a morning resistance-training group and a separate midday workout team of three for hot isometrics. In our small midday group, we do a HOT-WORX® infrared workout at 11:30 a.m. almost every day of the workweek. This is usually a 30-minute isometric workout. Some days we do a 15-minute hot HIIT workout inside the infrared sauna immediately following 30 minutes of hot isometrics. The boost in energy for the rest of the workday is incredible! If your company does not offer this type of workout opportunity, request it now from your HR department. Better productivity means higher revenues for your organization.

> **Do it for yourself, too. More productivity can get you higher commissions, or a promotion, or both! The only true form of job security is job performance—never forget that!**

If you're looking for a better workout schedule, try 30 minutes of infrared isometrics three to four times per week with friends for lunch. I can tell you that, for myself and my colleagues, we all swear by the lunchtime HOTWORX® workouts. Whenever you prefer to schedule your workout, there are some great advantages to a small-group infrared workout routine, including:

Motivation

It has been proven scientifically that working out with others elevates your intensity. I know this is true from experience with my lunchtime workout team and from my more recently formed weight-training workout team with two of my best friends and fitness colleagues, Jerome Price and Jeremy Harwell, for 7:30 a.m. Mondays through Fridays at the office gym. We call ourselves the "Wrecking Krewe" (in keeping with our New Orleans hometown roots for the spelling of *crew*). Camaraderie definitely increases your motivation.

Reduced Stress, Increased Energy

I recommend the lunchtime workout because halfway through the workday for a busy executive is a good time to practice stress management and to accelerate energy levels. From the moment you walk into the HOTWORX® sauna, stress begins to go away, and when the workout begins, your energy is mobilized both mentally and physically. When you are finished with the workout, the fist bumps of workout success are made with your colleagues, and you go back to work with a new attitude for the rest of the day.

Workout Variety

With multiple isometric workouts to choose from, a different HOT-WORX® lunchtime workout can be experienced each day. It's very effective to cross-train day to day from Hot ISO to Hot Yoga to Hot Pilates, Hot Buns, etc. The variety of isometric workouts helps to cross-strengthen all your muscles, and it also yields improvements to exercise that you might do outside of HOTWORX®, such as weight training, outdoor cycling, snow skiing, and running.

Decreased Appetite

Our lunchtime infrared workouts usually begin at 11:30, which is perfect for helping to reduce your lunchtime appetite. Following a minimal breakfast, such as one protein drink combined with morning supplements only, some trainers call this midday, pre-meal (before lunch) routine a "fasted" approach to the workout. Many trainers will recommend fasted cardio workouts. Fasted workouts can help you to burn more fat. HOTWORX® isometrics is, without a doubt, a great cardio workout, and it will be a workout while your body is in a fasted state if you eat an early, low-calorie breakfast with no snacks before the lunchtime workout. Keep your breakfast moderate, and don't eat again until after your lunchtime workout.

The infrared workout helps to reduce hunger and causes you to want less food for lunch. I always experience this effect with a lunchtime workout. According to David Stensel, PhD, "Exercise may lower levels of ghrelin, a hormone that stimulates appetite in the short term while raising levels of peptide YY, a hormone that suppresses appetite."[1]

Finally, having an infrared HOTWORX® workout for lunch with your friends is just plain awesome for your personal work results—and as a CEO, that is productivity music to my ears!

1. "Exercise Can Curb Hunger, New Research Finds," Today.com, September 15, 2011, https://www.today.com/news/exercise-can-curb-hunger-new-research-finds-wbna 44523397.

PART III

Getting the Most From Your HOTWORX® Workout

"If you can conceive it and believe it,

then go do it and achieve it!"

Chapter 14

HOTWORX® Mind + Body = Power

A **FITNESS PROGRAM SHOULD BE** designed for one reason. That reason is RESULTS. Focus on your fitness goals and use the program as a tool for results. The practice of mental and physical connection through awareness is essential for optimal results. It is a mistake to view the body as separate from the mind. The whole is always greater than the parts viewed independently. True power in fitness comes when the mind and the body are seen as one.

Find a fitness center that values and fosters the Mind + Body = Power equation.

I am appalled by gyms that allow and even encourage behavior such as staff providing Tootsie Rolls to clients, or pizza parties. I have even seen YouTube videos of members eating sandwiches while sitting on a workout machine. What is that? Sorry, but a fitness center should BE a fitness center, a health club should BE a health club—a place for results and not a $10 per month slot machine with no hope to win the fitness jackpot. The only path to the fitness jackpot is through mindful dedication to results. Results, my friend. It's about results for your mind and body!

Without a doubt, the first priority in your quest for a high-level workout is to place yourself into the proper results-oriented environment. Most people are aware of the notion that a mind/body connection is beneficial in some way. However, most people have no idea what it really means or how it benefits a fitness program.

Mind + body as one can be a powerful way to get you to the best workout results of your life.

It begins with this simple truth: you get what you focus on. When you focus your attention on what your body is doing during your workout, then you will perform better, and your results will be greater. The more often you practice high-level mental focus on your muscles and movement, the stronger you will become. You will absolutely gain more strength quicker if you begin to view the mind and the body as one.

Envision high levels of focus and determination just before your workouts. Rid your mind of daily stress and focus on your workout. Never forget that the workout environment can make or break the mind/body connection.

One of the reasons we created the HOTWORX® workout sauna was to provide a tool to help workout focus. Inside the infrared sauna, the setting is private, intimate, and designed for no more than three clients. With the infrared energy and heat at 125°F, enhancing the ability to be present at the moment for all your workouts, your training sets will be more engaging. Your mental connection with your body movement in these small-group training sessions will always be higher than that of open, air-conditioned workout rooms packed with too many people.

I am reminded of one of my off-season coaches who helped me

train for arena football. Coach Duke used to always tell us to "get your mind right" to keep us focused on what our bodies were doing. Rather than just showing up for a workout and going through the motions, make a conscious effort to bring your level of awareness up to connect your thoughts with the movements of your body! Focus your thoughts inward and about your muscles doing the work. Zone in on balance and form. Your brain sends signals to your muscles, and you should ensure that there is no distraction for this connection.

Yoga is one of the most effective methods of exercise to foster a mind/body connection. Yoga requires an incredible amount of focus, and hot yoga can take it to another level. Yoga postures force you to concentrate on balance, which requires mental presence. Other forms of isometrics work well too for this purpose. It takes a full-on awareness of the mind in connection to the muscle to hold a balancing isometric posture.

With the HOTWORX® yoga workout, immediately after the modified sun salutation warm-up, we open the posture sequence with eagle pose. Eagle is a good example of an exercise that requires a high level of mind/body connection for balance and power in a posture that is held over an extended amount of time. Power, according to *Webster's*, is the ability to act or produce an effect. So, for more power to move and to deliver fitness results to yourself, practice the integration of mind and body!

Experience more fitness power when your mind and body work together as one.

Chapter 15

Getting Motivated to
HOTWORX®

MOTIVATION IS FUNDAMENTAL to working out. Working out requires work, and work requires motion. You have to get off the couch to do the work! You can always do more than you think you can do, and now is the time to get yourself in motion! What is the thing that can stimulate you toward action?

BELIEVE...

The foundation of motivation is belief. There's no argument against that. In fitness, to achieve your goals, it certainly starts with the belief that you can. As a fitness professional, nothing is more upsetting than to listen to someone saying they need to "think about it" before they begin a fitness program. What is there to think about? Choose to BELIEVE that you can and begin that program today! Stop procrastinating. A good friend of mine and the "guru" of fitness membership recruitment, as I call him, John Paul Yersick, or "JP," once told me that the sworn enemy of achievement is procrastination. In my view, procrastination is just a fancy word for laziness. Don't be lazy!

DO...

The next step is to actually DO SOMETHING! Take action. Find the program that will be the most effective tool to get you to your goal in a safe, timely, and efficient manner. "Do" consistently and use a method that will allow you to measure progress.

As a trainer, one of my biggest pet peeves is the trend toward, let's call it hyper-variety of types of exercises within any one fitness genre. How can you measure progress if you are told to do a different workout with different exercises every time you come to the gym? That is bad advice. Just know that you need to DO a program consistently every week and stay within a reasonable pattern of "sameness."

ACHIEVE...

If you DO a routine with relentless regularity, then you will get to the next step, which is to ACHIEVE the results that you want. Don't bask in the glory for too long, though.

Now it's time to REPEAT.
BELIEVE, DO, ACHIEVE . . . REPEAT.

This is the fitness cycle of success, for sure. It sounds so easy, but we all know better. It's simple, but not easy. Of course, as the old saying goes, "Nothing in life worth having is easy." True that! Just keep repeating to yourself, BELIEVE, DO, ACHIEVE, over and over again.

Never stop!

Chapter 16

Setting HOTWORX® Goals

YOUR **"FITNESS WEAPON"** is a four-letter word. That four-letter word is a big, audacious G-O-A-L! Nothing is more motivating. Yet, no matter the fitness program, there will always be those who perform at a higher level of effort, intensity, and focus. If you ask those people why they work harder, they will most likely tell you that they are getting ready for something. That something is usually either a sports competition/event, a vacation, or a combination of the two. For the highest level of motivation, I recommend a combination of the two!

Now, think about when you are most productive with your fitness routine, and consider the following questions from the legendary motivator Zig Ziglar.

> As an honest, intelligent person, do you, as a general rule, get about twice as much work done on the day before you go on vacation as you normally get done? . . . If we can figure out why and learn how and repeat it every day without working any longer or any harder, does it make sense that we will be more valu-

able to ourselves, our company, our family, and our community? The answer is, "Yes."[1]

Zig Ziglar says:

"Treat every day like it's the day before vacation, and you will get more work done!"

Let's think about what Ziglar has to say and apply it to our workouts. If we can work out every time we are in the gym or the studio like it is the day before vacation, then think of how our level of fitness will soar. I believe the key to this workout mentality is to choose a "fitness weapon" for motivation. It could be a 5K run or an obstacle course. You may prefer to train for a yoga retreat, a hike to the top of a mountain, or a hike to the bottom of the Grand Canyon. Your fitness weapon is your goal, and your goal is limited only by your imagination! Set it, go for it, and think about it every day until you are there.

I have found that the thought of ski runs on certain mountains provides me with high levels of training motivation. I think about those runs when I do HOTWORX®, or when I am weight training or when I run stadiums. Your fitness weapon is personal, but it can be shared with others. Train with your friends to get ready for a fitness retreat or some other vacation that involves physical activity.

Use the vision of your activities on vacation as your fitness weapon for motivation.

1. Zig Ziglar, "How to Get More Work Done in a Day," accessed May 22, 2020, http://www.getmotivation.com/articlelib/articles/zziglar_more_done.htm.

Personal Goals

The vision of snow skiing, or hiking a ski mountain in the summer, is one of my most effective personal motivational tools. My ski trips are planned and then used as my personal fitness GOAL! I am also beginning to plan summer cycling and/or hiking trips as well. If I am weight training or if I am working out in the HOTWORX® infrared workout sauna, I am in constant training for my next ski trip, or hike! That's me. For you, it might be the same, or it might be a surfing vacation or a trip that involves scuba diving or paddle boarding, a yoga retreat, or some other physical activity.

I have always believed that for anyone to achieve a balance in life, some sort of physical fitness goal has to be a part of the equation. For me, now that my bodybuilding and football days have passed, that physical fitness goal has changed to quality snow skiing for the most part. I work to improve my physical fitness to up the "quality" of my snow skiing game. Skiing is the most fun that I can have while achieving a high level of quality exercise at the same time. Of late, though, I have added hiking to the mix.

My most recent fitness vacation did involve a mountain, but not for skiing. Rather, this mountain, the Gros Piton in Saint Lucia, which originally attracted my attention for its sheer beauty, became the object of my passion for fitness. Years ago, I remember admiring and then tearing out a magazine picture of Sugar Beach, which is nestled between the two volcanic Piton mountains. These two mountains comprise the smaller Petite Piton and the larger Gros Piton. I taped that magazine page to my washing machine to remind me that one day I would go to Sugar Beach to experience the beauty of that island in person.

It wasn't until recent years that my Saint Lucia thoughts turned to wondering what it would be like to climb the Gros Piton. Those thoughts turned into a new fitness goal to scale the Gros Piton. With that new goal in mind, I set out to create a business objective that would allow my colleagues and I, along with our significant others, to travel to Saint Lucia for a corporate vacation retreat. We did indeed accomplish the business objective and earn the trip, sending us down there to that beautiful island in December 2019.

I invited the entire group to climb the mountain. When it came time for the hike, there were four of us who stepped up for the challenge—me, my girlfriend Brittany, my great friend and HOTWORX® business coach Jeremy Harwell (the original manager of the first HOTWORX® location in Oxford, MS), and one of my best friends for many years Jerome Price (who is also the husband of my business partner Nancy).

I often train at HOTWORX® with Brittany, and I can always rely on her for a great infrared workout. Jeremy, Jerome, and I constitute the "Wrecking Krewe," which is our morning weight-training group that I spoke of earlier in the book.

Jerome agreed to hike up to a point and then wait for the rest of us to climb to the top and come back down. Jerome battles with a lingering back injury

So, we decided to take a boat from the small village of Soufriere to the beach at the foot of the Gros Piton to begin our trek. We wanted to scale the entirety of the mountain from the beach to the top. Most of the hikers begin from the end of a road that leads to a beginning point about a quarter of the way up the mountain, which is cheating, in my opinion. Normally, according to most accounts, it takes four hours from that abbreviated point to hike up and then back down to that same point. Very few Gros Piton climbers begin from the true base of the mountain, which is at the beach.

We scaled that mountain from the beach to top (2,618.9ft) and back down to the beach in four hours and 13 minutes. The climb took us up a makeshift trail that consisted of dirt paths, steep rocks, railings (where there was railing) made of branches that were randomly nailed together, trees, giant roots, vines, and stumps, along with many other winding obstacles and crude manmade steps. I burned an incredible 2,769 calories during that climb. We all agreed that it was the best HIIT workout of our life thus far! What a rush it was to get to the top.

The accomplishment of a fitness goal is always fun.

So, I practice weight training and HOTWORX® to improve my skiing and hiking. If I have better skills, then I have more fun on the slopes, and to me, that is the greatest natural high ever! Planning for a good ski trip or a great hiking excursion is a super motivator for my fitness routine.

I always set a specific date for the next fitness vacation. Then, I ready myself with weight training and HOTWORX®. When I finally get to the vacation destination, it's GOAL time!

The use of a physical fitness goal that involves a sport-related vacation can supremely elevate your workout program.

Ready, set, GOAL your way to top-notch fitness!

Chapter 17

Go for Consistency with HOTWORX®

WE ADHERE TO THE fundamental workout principle of CONSISTENCY because muscles strengthen most efficiently from practice through a logical training sequence. Therefore, the choreography and production of each HOTWORX® workout type pay special attention to the consistency of flow and postures for isometrics, and consistency of intervals for HIIT. This is a vital component to provide for performance measurability and to accelerate the progression of strength and skill. Muscles respond to signals and cannot be shocked or confused. Muscle strength is gained through training method consistency.

To alleviate boredom, cross-training is the proper way to go to obtain workout variety. Cross-training is not to be confused with CrossFit (CrossFit is a workout method that employs the heavy use of plyometrics). Cross-training is the use of multiple workout types to enhance the performance of each workout type.

Cross-training incorporates the use of multiple workout types within the same day or the same week of a workout routine. Cross-training is a vital component of the HOTWORX® method, and it alleviates boredom that can be caused by the practice of only one workout type. Cross-training keeps motivation high and promotes the work of different muscles, and different work for the same muscles, which elevates your performance for each consistent workout type you practice. Cross-training allows for multiple sets of muscles to be worked and strengthened rather than only the muscles that are worked from the practice of a single workout type. We encourage the practice of multiple workout types such as programs that combine the use of yoga, Pilates, and indoor cycle HIIT along with others that work together and form a personal workout regimen.

In a nutshell:

- The practice of performing the same workout type differently every day is less safe, is less effective, and is not a part of the HOTWORX® method.
- The practice of performing a different workout type every day of the week or within the same day, so long as the workout type has consistency, is more effective.
- Cross-training diversifies the training program while retaining workout-type consistency, accelerates progression, and motivates.
- When combined with the elements of heat and infrared energy, cross-training creates fitness routines that are faster and that deliver more results.

Measurable Results

Without workout consistency in fitness, it becomes very difficult to measure performance progress. In business, performance progress measurement is vital to the success of the organization. Business performance is measured simply to a standard set for the same business unit in the previous month or in the same month for the previous year.

Business progress is also measured by comparing results to industry standards. The same logic applies to individual fitness programs. For example, if a particular workout calls for a 2.5-minute plank, then you will perform the exercise to a level. When you do the exact same plank for the same 2.5 minutes three days later, chances are you will be stronger, and you will perform at a higher level with better form and with less effort. It is easy to measure your performance when there is consistency with your workout routines.

Conversely, if your trainer calls for you to do a different exercise every single time that you work out, then how do you measure your progress? What will you measure it against? Find a new trainer who values consistency.

VARIETY OF WORKOUTS = GOOD. CONSTANT CHANGE WITHIN THOSE WORKOUTS = NOT SO GOOD.

It is certainly okay, and even advisable most of the time, to do different types of workouts during your week so long as those workouts remain consistent with their instructor cueing and flow of exercises. HOTWORX® 24 Hour Infrared Fitness Studios provide multiple types of isometric workouts and HIIT workouts that remain consistent. The workouts that need to be revised are upgraded every six months, and on an as-needed basis but remain true to the flow of exercises so members can always measure their performance consistently.

Consistency provides a rock-solid workout foundation.

Within consistency, there are plenty of opportunities to experience variety as you progress within a workout routine. How? As your strength, balance, endurance, and form improve, through the process of improvement, your muscles will discover and learn new movement. You should seek to learn new movement through cross-training. Learning requires an openness to a variety of consistent movement and a commitment to trial and error. The discovery of a new movement within the disciplines of consistent workout types is the most important variable to seek. I would caution you, do not seek out variety from different exercises in every set within only one workout type. Workouts should be consistent, not chaotic.

When you begin to practice consistent workout routines, you will easily see yourself making gains. Keeping it simple with consistency is powerful in terms of motivation, too. Consistency provides for easy progress measurement, and constant progress is the best workout reinforcement there is.

Some 15 years ago, I began a one-on-one training program with a football coach to prepare myself for an opportunity to play arena football. I trained for a year and a half to get ready. I went to meet Coach Turner at New Orleans City Park's outdoor training track-and-field facilities for the 90-minute sessions three times per week. Coach Turner knew the right mix of consistent drills and exercises to allow for my progress to be measured. When it came time for the actual football training camp in Columbus, Georgia, I showed up in the best shape of my life at the age of 41. My improved skills and excellent conditioning was all due to the consistent training methods that Coach Turner had introduced me to. If it works for football, then you can rest assured that it works for general fitness!

The HOTWORX® Workout Method takes a logical and measured approach to revisions for each of the workout types that are offered both for hot isometrics and hot HIIT. HOTWORX® has discovered through experience that workout-type revisions are best when they are done on a biannual basis. Therefore, new workout videos are produced every six months for most of the isometric and HIIT routines. The biannual productions incorporate subtle changes and tweaks to improve the workout flows and postures for hot yoga, hot Pilates, and all the other isometric-based workouts, and small revisions are made as well to the HIIT routines. These revisions, though, are not overdone and always remain consistent to allow for measurability. Subtle changes are made, if necessary, in terms of postures and sequencing within the flows, and new virtual instructors are introduced when needed to keep the sessions fresh while remaining consistent with the HOTWORX® workout method.

Remain consistent, my friends, and track your progress if you want to obtain the greatest results from your fitness program!

Chapter 18

Timing and Tracking with HOTWORX®

THE PHRASE "TIMING IS EVERYTHING" is relevant to almost every life endeavor, from athletics to cooking, and from comedy to rocket launches and political campaigns. So whether you believe in the phrase or not, certainly we can all recognize that timing is involved in everything.

Consistency, repetition, and discipline are all measured by intervals of time. Heart rate, one of the most important fitness indicators, is a measurement of the number of beats within a specified time. Proper timing is the key to success in fitness, as in life. Manifest your fitness destiny by taking control of your personal timing!

You can do this by taking control of your workouts with proper timing and taking the time to make the positive choice of the right fitness programs, and when you do, remember these words of wisdom from one great American poet, Ralph Waldo Emerson:

"This time, like all times, is a very good one if we but know what to do with it."

FX Zone

We recently launched a simple new tool for our members to use in our functional training area known as the FX Zone. The FX Zone serves as an area where members can supplement their hot exercise workouts with non-heated functional training. Functional training incorporates exercises that work to enhance everyday human movements such as bending over to pick up a book. Doing reps within a specified interval of time works well when used with functional training exercises.

In addition to our FX Zone silent trainer video, TV monitors in every studio display a 30-second revolving interval timer, 24/7, so you can practice functional interval training without having to look at your wristwatch or phone. The FX Zone timer is a simple, highly visible tool to allow for rest and workout intervals in any combination of 30-second multiples. This is yet another tool to increase the level of convenience and motivation for HOTWORX® Studio members.

Make the most out of every timing interval that you commit to! Your fitness depends on it.

Battle Rope Intervals

Every HOTWORX® 24 Hour Infrared Fitness Studio franchise equips the functional training area FX Zone with one or two fitness "battle ropes," which are anchored to the floor. Appropriately termed, battle ropes most likely evolved from ropes used by the ships of the world down through the history of naval warfare. You can just imagine hardworking sailors on the decks of these ships grasping heavy ropes to help maneuver sails and to assist in docking the vessels at port. Without a doubt, the swinging and fastening of those true battle ropes must have called for incredible physical force and manpower.

No wonder that modern-day fitness has found a way to utilize this ancient naval practice to make for great workouts. Battle ropes can offer you a great addition to your functional workout. There are countless combinations of techniques that can be applied to their use. They utilize the force of gravity with the force of the anchored ropes themselves for a powerful wave-movement combination.

Hand coordination and posture are keys to a successful battle rope set. The rope training allows you to utilize wave force, engaging your body to respond by adapting to the motions of the ropes.

"It's a little like running with the upper body," said Jonathan Ross, spokesperson for the American Council on Exercise. "It's not just using different muscles but training muscles in different ways."[1]

Battle ropes are great for arms, shoulders, and back, and with proper form, the squat position works the lower body as well, especially the glutes. Another big advantage of ropes is that there is a very low risk of injury, specifically as compared with plyometrics and weight training with barbells.

Battle rope intervals are a form of HIIT, assuming that you keep your intensity level up. I recommend 30-second high-intensity intervals for ropes. This is great for burning calories. Keep in mind that high-intensity interval training creates more after-workout calorie burn because of the increased recovery of oxygen needs. Ropes create a higher metabolic demand on your body and therefore a higher energy expenditure, which is a good tactic for a weight-loss strategy.[2]

So show yourself the ropes. Your fitness routine will thank you.

1. Dorene Intenicola, "'Battle Ropes' Could Be the Next Trendy Workout," Business Insider, May 25, 2015, http://www.businessinsider.com/r-battle-ropes-become-popular-go-to-fitness-tools-in-us-gyms-2015-5.

2. Aaron Guyett, "5 Benefits of Battle Ropes Training," Onnit, October 3, 2016, updated February 24, 2019, https://www.onnit.com/academy/5-benefits-of-battle-ropes-training/.

As of the publishing of this book, we are launching a new feature to our FX Zone, a Virtual Personal Training (VPT) program that will be accessible to members through the HOTWORX® Burn Off App. This program features two virtual personal trainers who lead the user through workouts in the FX Zone. The workouts are segmented by body parts.

The FX Zone was originally designed for and is still used as a functional training area with a "silent trainer video" that plays continuously on one monitor along with an interval timer monitor to assist clients with their workout sets. Now, with our upgraded Sweat Everywhere membership, you can use the Virtual Personal Trainer (VPT) in your HOTWORX® Burn Off App for a specific body part training. Users can select the body part that they want to train then select the trainer that they want from the options to the right of the body part, and then they can proceed with the workout video. Members can start and pause when necessary as they move through the workout. They watch and listen and follow their VPT for proper form and other training techniques.

We created a new product known as the HOTWORX® Phone Caddy and offer wireless headphones to assist members with the VPT program. Wireless headphones are required with the VPT program so as not to distract fellow members in the FX Zone and to keep things personal between the client and their VPT.

Stay tuned, there is more to come from this groundbreaking new functional workout program in the future.

Tracking

Studies have shown that people who use fitness trackers become more active. In business, we know how important it is to inspect what you expect. There's nothing more motivating than an impending inspection from a supervisor or knowing that a customer can give you a review for the world to see at any time when you own a business. The same accountability holds true for your level of fitness.

If you expect to get in shape, then you will need to inspect your progress. Accountability motivates!

At some point in your fitness journey, you should consider making key-data fitness tracking an important component to help you reach beyond your current fitness level. Keep in mind that many fitness tracking devices on the market can help you, but you should pay close attention to accuracy and choose your device accordingly. Generally, heart rate is measured accurately by reputable devices such as Apple Watch and Fitbit. Still, calorie measurement requires algorithms that are created based on proxy factors and a method incorporated by the creator. Therefore, you should choose your device wisely. We recommend that you select a device from a well-known and respected brand. One researcher from Stanford in a recent study of fitness tracking accuracy makes the point that it is very difficult to create a one-size-fits-all algorithm that would be accurate for all people. Calorie tracking, which is a measure of energy expenditure, depends on many variables including an individual's height and weight, fitness level, etc.[3]

Generally, heart rate data is reliable with devices that use blood-motion light sensors, but energy-expenditure (calorie-burn) accuracy is less reliable. Again, my advice is to invest in a tracker from one of the major brands that have good reputations, such as Apple Watch, Fitbit, Garmin, or Polar. And don't be lulled into a focus on passive fitness data such as step tracking. Just tracking steps is not enough. So, when you purchase your fitness device, what should you do next? This question is what prompted HOTWORX® to create a "key" fitness data set with a simple fitness tracking method.

3. Jennie Dusheck, "Fitness Trackers Accurately Measure Heart Rate but Not Calories Burned," Stanford Medicine News Center, May 24, 2017, https://med.stanford.edu/news/all-news/2017/05/fitness-trackers-accurately-measure-heart-rate-but-not-calories-burned.html.

"Our survey suggests—and experts we spoke with agree—
that you should view trackers as one tool in a
comprehensive effort to be more active, lose weight,
and improve your health."[4]

That *Consumer Reports* quote is spot on. Understand that your new fitness tracker is just a tool. Fitness tracking needs to be comprehensive but not complicated. All you need is a trusted fitness watch, a body-fat calculator, and a scale to track your fitness data.

When we set about devising a tracking app, our aim was to keep things simple. Many data points can be used to track fitness. The items that needed to be addressed were what are the most vital stats to compile, and what is the simplest way to track them in a gym or studio setting? That two-part question provided the motivation for us to create a better data tracking method through an app and eventually that would have syncing capability with Apple Watch and Fitbit.

Arguably, the most relevant sets of data for most fitness
programs include calories, body fat, and body weight.

To create a user-friendly method for tracking this data, it takes an app that can work with any fitness device so long as that device has a heart rate monitor and an easily accessible (and viewable) data screen. High-quality, brand-name wrist devices work the best and have better reputations for accuracy. The HOTWORX® Burn Off App works with any device but will automatically sync with the Apple Watch and with Fitbit.

Of course, the HOTWORX® Burn Off App is another timing tool

---

4. Brendan Borrell, "Precise Devices: Fitness Trackers Are More Accurate Than Ever," *Consumer Reports*, June 29, 2017, https://www.consumerreports.org/fitness-trackers/precise-devices-fitness-trackers-are-more-accurate-than-ever/.

and can be used for calorie calculations during the length of the workout(s) and during the hour after-burn. Also, the 90-day challenge lets you see where you stack up against other members who are app users. The app challenges you to achieve higher levels of performance and resets every 90 days to allow for constant measurement against that specific amount of time. With the HOTWORX® Burn Off App, there is always a new 90-day challenge!

HOTWORX® Key-Data Fitness Tracking Method

Here is how it works:

1. Purchase and learn how to use a quality fitness wrist device for heart-rate monitoring and calories burned.
2. Join a HOTWORX® 24 Hour Infrared Fitness Studio, then download the mobile fitness Burn Off App.
3. Use the Burn Off App with your fitness watch and mobile phone to track the workout calories and hour workout after-burn data for every workout at the studio.
4. Use the body-fat testing device (provided at HOTWORX® Studios 24/7) for body-fat percent and record the data with the Burn Off App photo method. Recording body fat monthly is usually the best test interval for body fat.
5. Use the scale to measure body weight once per week or once per month (or any time interval) and record the results with the Burn Off App photo method.

These vital fitness tracking measurements will provide you with a simple set of highly relevant fitness data in an easy-to-track format.

Chapter 19

Make HOTWORX® Your Wake-Up Call

THERE IS NO DOUBT that a great morning workout can elevate your day. Here are four good reasons to consider making morning the time for your daily exercise so that you can get the most out of your HOTWORX® routine.

- **Morning workouts improve your discipline.** When your discipline improves, you may find that you eat healthier meals, prioritize punctuality, and begin to form more productive habits.
- **Exercising in the morning kick-starts your energy level for the day.**
- **A morning workout turns up your brainpower.** Studies have shown that a morning workout is better than coffee for starting the day with high focus. I like both, actually, the morning workout with the morning coffee! In fact, studies show that a good workout prior to an important meeting or presentation can help to channel your focus and attention. I totally agree based on my own experience. Every year prior

to my company address at our franchise convention, I make
sure to get in an early morning workout about two hours pri-
or to the speech.

- **Sleep is better.** When you work out in the morning, there is
  a more logical daily fatigue pattern. When combined with
  infrared exposure, you can expect even deeper and longer
  sleep as a result of your early-day workouts.

If you want to double-jump-start your day, try breaking up your
workout into morning and lunch for a second energy boost. Here's
an idea: do hot isometrics in the morning and a 15-minute hot HIIT
for lunch! Your day will be awesome, and, again, you will sleep like a
baby.

A good 30-minute functional workout in the FX Zone, with ket-
tlebells and suspension straps, or weight training and ropes, works
well too for the morning wake-up call, combined with a lunchtime
infrared workout.

Chapter 20

HOTWORX® and the Power of Three

IT TAKES A SPECIAL PERSON who can achieve the highest level of motivation for a workout when training solo with no other people around. Even when training by yourself, you always achieve a higher level of performance if you have a trainer to push you or if you are simply in a workout environment such as a gym or a park where there are others around. It's human nature to want to perform at a higher level in front of people or with others close by! You know it's true.

There is evidence to prove this. There is research out there to suggest that working out in a group releases a rush of chemicals in the brain much like that of when you dance with others or when you laugh together. This is an important part of our human experience. Working out with "buddies could help turn fitness into a pleasant addiction,"[1] the *Globe and Mail* reported.

Most fitness centers now provide large- or small-group exercise programs with professional trainers and instructors. The demand for this type of exercise is very high because people work out harder in

---

1. Alex Hutchinson, "Is Group Exercise Better Than Working Out Solo?," *Globe and Mail*, January 6, 2010, updated May 12, 2018, http://www.theglobeandmail.com/life/health-and-fitness/fitness/is-group-exercise-better-than-working-out-solo/article4268232/.

a group and have more fun! Accountability is very important for any fitness program, and working out in a group can elevate this to a positive extreme. And when there is an instructor, things keep moving at a good pace with professional exercise queuing.

We kept this in mind when we designed the HOTWORX® fitness program. The HOTWORX® sauna has proven to be the most effective environment for small groups of three. This hot exercise sauna can service three clients for isometrics and HIIT. The small group of three is perfect for hot yoga, Pilates, and other forms of isometrics, and for HIIT with a cycle or row machine.

As a fitness trainer of small groups for many years, I found out through experience that three is the ideal number of clients to train together in a group. This is known as small-group training in the personal training business. My small groups ranged from one to 10, but most of the time, there were three to five clients. I quickly found that the perfect number for group accountability was three. With three during a workout, the clients always seemed to have more fun and train harder. I always enjoyed the groups of three over any other group size as a trainer, and I felt that the information I delivered was more directly consumed by a group of this size. A group of three allowed for better information exchange to and from the clients.

The camaraderie of this small-group workout makes for good company during the infrared sessions! Three is the perfect company for a fitness-training session.

Chapter 21

How to Hydrate for HOTWORX®

THE MORE YOU HYDRATE during a workout in the sauna, the more you sweat. The more you sweat, the more you detox. Make sure you hydrate properly. By that, I mean keep your sports drink shaker next to you, and drink plenty whenever you need to.

While utilizing an infrared sauna, you should make sure that you keep water on hand during the session. Drink at least 12fl oz during a 30-minute session, and replace electrolytes after your session with a good sports drink. If you prefer, you can drink electrolytes before, during, and after the sauna session as a part of your hydration method. I prefer to drink water with an electrolyte and amino acid powder mix so that nutrients your body needs are being supplied to your system along with the hydration. This is a 2-for-1 approach to hydration, nutrition + hydration.

Sweat composition varies per person. An average liter of sweat contains 20mg of calcium, 50mg magnesium, 1,150mg sodium, 230mg potassium, and 1,480mg chloride. Electrolyte replacement drinks should have these plus a small number of carbohydrates to aid in the electrolyte replacement process. Try a good sports drink. Gatorade and Powerade work well, or you can try a specialty powder formulation to mix in your sports drink shaker. PB Clean Energy is an excellent powder formulation for energy and for electrolytes as well as the HOTWORX® Pre and Post Workout Powders containing amino acids as well, which can be mixed with water.

The revolutionary new HOTWORX® infrared/isometric and HIIT workout program provides an excellent workout at 125°F for a 30- or 15-minute session. With any type of workout, it is important to hydrate properly while training. It is especially important to hydrate properly when exercising in an infrared sauna because of the accelerated sweating. Make sure to keep plenty of water and/or a sports drink by your workout mat, and hydrate to enhance the effectiveness of your session.

If you are an owner or manager of a fitness facility, make sure that you have quality bottled water and a good option for an electrolyte replacement beverage, as well as pre- and post-workout powders to mix with water for sale.

Efficient Hydration for Before, During, and Post-workout

One point that is not impressed upon enough by trainers and fitness writers is the advantage of mixing pre- and post-workout supplements with water for your workout hydration needs. Proper hydration and supplementation are super important for infrared training or any other form of physical training.

It makes good sense to give your body what it needs when it needs it before, during, and after your workout. This is even more important for infrared workouts because of the accelerated rate of sweating and energy expenditure during hot exercise. Make sure that you hydrate properly and mix the right supplements with water to consume before exercise and during/after exercise.

Remember this. Your body needs more than just water during workouts.

That is why I recommend mixing supplement powders with water for good pre-workout hydration and a good post-workout powder for use during and immediately after workouts.

Of course, there are tons of supplement brands out there touting the benefits of their pre- and post-workout pills, powders, and drinks. I have tried many of them and have noticed that they have a wide variation in results. I use our own HydroGo Powders by HOTWORX® now because of the precise formulations.

Pre-workout Hydration

Pre-workout products are designed primarily as an energy supplement. From my experience with pre-workout supplements, the energy effect is different for each formulation. Some of these products create a jittery effect rather than the more desirable feeling of smooth alertness.

If you feel that you need an energy boost, try a good pre-workout powder mixed with water about 30 minutes before exercise. A good pre-workout supplement will include ingredients such as natural caffeine from green tea leaf combined with taurine. Some studies suggest that taurine, in conjunction with caffeine, helps to improve cognitive functioning. Taurine is an amino acid that, as studies have indicated, can act as an antioxidant to counteract free radicals and may enhance athletic performance.

Post-workout Hydration

Whether you choose to use a good pre-workout powder or not, it is imperative to invest in a good post-workout powder for use during workouts and immediately after workouts to achieve the maximum hydration effect and to assist in workout recovery.

Assisting with Muscle Recovery

As you work out, you break down muscle. A good workout powder mixed with water can immediately address this by supplying your muscle cells with the branched-chain amino acids necessary to immediately assist in muscle recovery and to supercharge the strength-building process.

What are branched-chain amino acids? Three out of the nine essential amino acids are branched-chain amino acids (BCAAs). BCAAs are found in high-protein foods such as meat, dairy products, and eggs.

BCAAs, when consumed, immediately begin to decrease muscle damage, and studies have shown that they can actually decrease post-workout soreness. They have also been shown to decrease fatigue related to workouts. BCAAs have also been successful in hospitals for reducing or stopping muscle loss in patients and for the treatment of liver disease.

The practice of mixing good pre- and post-workout powders for consumption before, during, and after your workouts can make a big difference in your workout performance and fitness results!

Give your body what it needs WHEN it needs it!

Chapter 22

Aromatherapy and HOTWORX®

AROMATHERAPY HAS BEEN USED as a form of medicine for centuries, with records dating back to ancient times. Aromatherapy is the use of plant-based essential oils to improve mind and body functions. The scent of properly mixed and released essential oil blends can have positive effects on a workout, especially a hot exercise session in a sauna. You have to try it to understand the uplifting experience. Essential oil scents can be used to elevate your emotional state before, during, and after your workout session. It has the effect of increasing awareness and improving workout focus, not to mention the improved scent of your workout space.

Whenever I use them, I notice an immediate heightening of the senses, and it really enhances the sauna environment. I also notice my increased level of motivation to keep pushing and holding, or cycling and sweating. Below is a description of my favorite workout "space and body" spray:

The HOTWORX® Space and Body Spray contains a blend of purified water, pure essential oil of tea tree (*Melaleuca Alternifolia*), pure essential oil of peppermint (*Menthe Arvensis*), pure essential oil of camphor (*Cinnamomum Camphora*), and an all-natural blend of honeydew melon, musk melon, watermelon, and cucumber. All you do is shake the small container well, hold in an upright position, and spray it on your yoga mat and towel and on your body before, during, and after yoga, or HIIT in the sauna. This product is great to use during any workout session and to freshen any room, workplace, or vehicle, too.

Of course, there are countless combinations of blends that can be experimented with to create a good essential oil workout scent. Tea tree, eucalyptus (make sure you are not allergic to eucalyptus), geranium, lemon, orange, peppermint, rosemary, black pepper, and lavender essential oils are good. Find your favorite scent and keep it in your gym bag or yoga bag to energize your workouts. Spray it on your skin when you are sweating, and be sure to keep it out of your eyes. Before training, spray it on your workout mat/towel and around your space inside the HOTWORX® infrared sauna.

You might also want to try adding a couple of drops of a citrus essential oil such as lemon to your workout water for increased hydration efficiency and better water taste.

Add a little aromatherapy for your next hot exercise session.

PART IV

HOTWORX® Exercise

"More workout, less time."

Chapter 23

HOTWORX® Cardio

DOING CARDIO IS HARD, and it can turn into a dull, boring grind if you keep doing it the old-school way—that is, by working endless minutes on the treadmill, elliptical, or stationary bike.

When I'm on the road, I like to train at as many different gyms as possible. I go to low-budget gyms and high-end clubs so that I can see firsthand what is happening throughout the industry. What I continue to see is lots of people frowning and drudging through their time on treadmills and other "monotonous" cardio equipment. This is not cool anymore, and it is not an effective use of your time. I see young professionals on the treadmill, and I want to tell them that there is a more efficient way to do cardio. Everyone should be informed that there is a way to get a lot more out of your cardio workout time.

Hey everybody, technology has paved the way now for a better way to do cardio. So why not combine strength training, flexibility, balance, and detox with your cardio workout for a quick, interesting, and fun session?

All you need is gravity, infrared, and a virtual instructor, and you can have a 3D Training experience. The by-product of this workout method is a fantastic cardio workout. I consistently reach 80-plus percent of my heart-rate max within the first five minutes of the workout and maintain that level throughout the rest of the 30-minute session. I always tell people that I never even think about cardio while I'm doing HOTWORX® isometrics. While I am focused on the isometrics, the cardio work just happens.

> **Strength + balance + flexibility + cardio training are all happening at once in this fast, multidimensional 30-minute workout!**

If you want to get the most out of your cardio training, leave the treadmill behind. Wave goodbye to it in your rearview mirror as you enter into the new frontier of infrared training.

Chapter 24

HOTWORX® Cross-Training

WE EXPLORED THE POWER OF cross-training for consistent variety in an earlier section and know that we made it a cornerstone component of the HOTWORX® training method when we created the first-ever 24 Hour Infrared Fitness Studio. As a professional trainer, I knew that we had to keep our individual workouts consistent and familiar to our customers while keeping things exciting for them with variety and options. Cross-training by practicing different types of workouts has been around for a long time, and it can provide stimulation for muscle development beyond just keeping to the same workout type every session.

There has been substantial research to demonstrate that people drop out of exercise programs, thanks to boredom. Common sense tells us that. Cross-training is the cure for workout boredom. It is safe, especially if it is based on low-to-zero-impact exercise such as the 3D Training Method from HOTWORX®. Cross-training can reduce the likelihood of injury, too, because it strengthens multiple muscle areas in the body. HOTWORX®, with over 10 workout types to choose from, provides unlimited opportunity for cross-training and adds to the injury prevention because of the zero-impact isometric and HIIT workouts that are offered. The isometrics are offered to provide for extensive and varied flexibility postures, as well as foam rolling to further lessen the chance for injury.

We have found from our membership data that the HOTWORX® Studio concept has an incredibly high exercise-adherence ratio as compared with industry standards. One of the reasons for this high level of repeat studio member visits is because of the opportunity to easily practice cross-training. HOTWORX® members can choose from a variety of 30-minute isometric workouts, two 15-minute HIIT workouts, and a complete functional training area called the FX Zone. There are endless combinations of ways to cross-train. Some members practice the Bonfire workout, which is a back-to-back workout session consisting of isometrics followed immediately by HIIT or vice versa! Some members simply schedule a different workout type every day of the week, for example:

Monday: Hot Yoga; **Tuesday:** Bonfire workout with Hot ISO and Hot Cycle back-to-back; **Wednesday:** Hot Warrior; **Thursday:** Hot Pilates; **Friday:** Bonfire Hot Core and Hot Blast.

There are thousands of ways to combine the workouts in the 24-hour HOTWORX® infrared fitness studio environment. The cross-training combinations are limited only by the imagination.

Keep the individual workouts consistent and cross-train for variety!

Chapter 25

HOTWORX® Yoga for Athletic Training and Fitness

GONE ARE THE DAYS OF coming into the gym to do bench press and dumbbell curls to call it a day. Modern fitness requires more specialized training and not for just one method, or "rut" routine if you will. Champion athletes always cross-train. They never allow themselves to plateau due to a stale, monotonous training routine. As defined in a *Runner's World* magazine article, "cross-training is when a runner trains by doing other fitness workouts—such as cycling, swimming, a fitness class, or strength training—to supplement their running. It builds strength and flexibility in muscles that running doesn't utilize. It prevents injury by correcting muscular imbalances. And the variety prevents boredom and burnout."[1]

Champions are always looking for a way to make gains and to push beyond their previous best. I recently discovered the Super Bowl XL-VIII champion Seattle Seahawks held mandatory yoga sessions as a part of their training regime leading up to their world championship

1. Andrew Enriquez, "Benefits of Group Exercise," Medical Center Health System, accessed May 22, 2020, https://mchodessa.com/fitness/benefits-of-group-exercise/.

win.[2] For a more specific football example, take a look at what Aaron Rodgers, quarterback for the Green Bay Packers, does to up his game. In addition to his traditional weight/resistance-training routine for football, he also practices yoga. *Men's Journal* magazine reported that Aaron Rodgers is "one of the fittest quarterbacks in the league." Rodgers combines weight training with suspension training and yoga.[3]

Rodgers made the following statement to the *Men's Fitness* journalist:

"I did a lot of stretching and yoga this offseason, which I have always felt has helped me to sustain my legs and my athleticism."[4]

Professional snowboarder Jamie Anderson, who won gold at the 2014 Olympics in Russia, credits a lot of her success to a disciplined yoga routine. In a *Yoga Journal* interview, she said, "It just gives me that ninja-like edge. And I feel strong and flexible, so I'm able to land better and crash better." She added, "If you're doing a lot of yoga, you should be happy! On and off your mat."[5]

Many HOTWORX® clients, amateur and pro athletes alike, use the 30-minute hot yoga and other isometrics along with the 15-minute hot HIIT workouts as supplemental training to enhance their athletic endeavors. These sports include activities like running, weight training, skiing, and rock climbing, to name a few. These amateur and pro athletes maintain their fundamental training practices of dynamic resistance in the forms of weight training and suspension training,

2. Andy Haley, "The 10 Best Yoga Poses for Athletes," Stack.com, updated February 10, 2019, https://www.stack.com/a/best-yoga-poses-for-athletes.

3. Matthew Jussim, "Aaron Rodgers Talks Offseason Training, Yoga, and Eating Habits: 'I Want to Play Another 10 Years,'" *Men's Journal*, accessed May 22, 2020, https://www.mensjournal.com/sports/aaron-rodgers-talks-offseason-training-yoga-and-eating-habits-i-want-play-another-10/.

4. Jussim, "Aaron Rodgers Talks Offseason Training, Yoga, and Eating Habits: 'I Want to Play Another 10 Years.'"

5. Jennifer D'Angelo Friedman, "Yoga for Snowboarders: Get the Ninja-Like Edge," *Yoga Journal*, updated April 5, 2017, https://www.yogajournal.com/practice/olympic-gold-medalist-snowboarder-jamie-anderson-yoga-trains-core-gives-ninja-like-edge.

but they supplement with hot infrared exercise to make progress in flexibility, balance, detoxification, and recovery, and even to make additional gains in strength.

Add some hot infrared yoga to your athletic training!

What about HOTWORX® Hot Yoga and general fitness?

No offense, but the days of Richard Simmons–style workouts have long passed. In the modern world, customers want more than old-school aerobics. People want more out of the time they have for fitness. People want more, and fitness professionals have responded with new and better workouts! Companies like HOTWORX® have responded to this demand with more efficient workout tools and routines.

As a result of this new fitness reality, the discipline of yoga has made a tremendous leap forward into the mainstream of the industry through many expanded methods and styles. One such method is a more fitness-oriented, athletic style of yoga.

As stated by wanderlust.com, "Yoga has shifted from being a form of physical therapy to being straight-up exercise."[6] Modern yoga forms such as that of HOTWORX® deliver more of a "Namaslay it" approach to yoga, giving clients therapy- and athletic-style exercise.

HOTWORX® yoga was created to meet the demands of the 21st-century fitness customer who wants "more workout in less time." HOTWORX® Hot Yoga incorporates a fast-paced, athletic style with active-recovery (due to heat and infrared energy) training sessions for beginners and advanced fitness enthusiasts alike. This yoga exercise sequence ensures a full-body isometric workout and utilizes virtual instructors who are always queuing clients to challenge themselves

---

6. Amanda Kohr, "The Difference between Athletic Yoga and Yoga for Athletes," Wanderlust, accessed May 22, 2020, https://www.wanderlust.com/journal/difference-athletic-yoga-yoga-athletes/.

and to go at their own best pace. With a well-choreographed exercise flow and virtual encouragement to work out at an appropriate pace and level of intensity, the session remains accessible to everyone who wishes to begin a yoga practice.

Athletes and average fitness club members use yoga as a tool to help them become better at their sport and for their general health to improve quality of life. However, HOTWORX®-style yoga promotes the mind/body connection and encourages extreme focus to improve balance and mental discipline. It also allows the muscles to process metabolic by-products at a faster rate due to the deep penetration of infrared energy at the cellular level. With HOTWORX® yoga, attention is given to power and strength along with the traditional flexibility, balance, and mental awareness. This is a more athletic, yet still holistic, approach to yoga that is better suited for exercise, everyday movement, and athletic performance.

HOTWORX® Hot Yoga enables clients to torch the calories, increase flexibility, improve endurance, and prevent injury as a supplement to other programs or as a standalone workout regime. Who wants to be stronger? This new infrared yoga style is also good for athletes or beginners who want to gain strength with increased heat shock protein synthesis due to heat acclimation.

Another yoga trend that is here to stay is the advent of private and semi-private training sessions. Yes, that's right, yoga personal training sessions. Through its use of virtual instruction, this is an area where HOTWORX® is leading the way with semi-private yoga training with groups of three people per infrared session. This is small-group training at its finest. The virtual training ensures that the yoga sessions are delivered on time and with proper flow and queuing for every workout!

With HOTWORX® yoga, customers can take advantage of working with a private virtual instructor in small groups of three and use a flexible scheduling system that is personalized through the HOT-WORX® Burn Off App appointment scheduling module.

Yoga has evolved! It's time to try it in an infrared sauna.

Chapter 26

HOTWORX® Hot Yoga Studio Difference

As **YOU KNOW** from part I, heated workouts in the form of hot yoga have been around for half a century, and those hot yoga sessions have been delivered almost exclusively inside studios heated with conventional HV/AC equipment. This type of environment is loud from the heater fans and stuffy from the hot air that is being blown everywhere. Furthermore, this old-school heat only warms the outside of the human body to cause sweat. It's literally just hot air.

Infrared heaters make no sound. Rather, the heat and energy simply radiate from the source. The silence of the heaters and the fact that the heat and energy are being absorbed by the human subject provide for a much better workout environment. As stated before, it has been proven that IR sauna heating is seven times more effective for detoxing than that of a conventional sauna or hot yoga studio.

Some yoga studios have attempted to create infrared hot yoga environments but have fallen short on heat effectiveness because they failed to understand the importance of precise IR heat source placement and proximity to their clients.

Every Detail Matters

The position of the infrared heaters is a feature that is of paramount importance to the patented sauna design.

This is worth repeating again because of the misinformation circulating throughout the hot yoga community with respect to infrared heat. When I was designing the HOTWORX® infrared workout sauna, it quickly became clear to me that to deliver an effective dose of infrared absorption to the human body, the subject must be exposed to the heat and energy source with very precise schematic considerations. For the proper penetration of infrared waves through the skin of the human body, the infrared heat and energy must be dispersed in a way that allows you to receive the most efficient infrared wave penetration through the skin. This requires the usage of different types of heaters placed in the right areas of the workout environment to spread the infrared throughout the space properly for clients.

Air Control

With yoga, especially, breathing is such an important aspect of the workout. Of course, proper breathing is important for all fitness routines, but the practice of yoga places great emphasis on breathing techniques. To date, however, HOTWORX® is the only hot yoga provider to pay such close attention to the quality of the air that is actually being breathed by clients while working out, and not just the technique of how they are breathing it.

Most hot yoga and hot Pilates studios use traditional heating methods that simply heat the air in the room. As stated earlier in the book, the original hot workout room was meant to re-create the climate in India, where yoga originated, at around 104°F and 40 percent humidity. While one could understand the intent to recreate where a workout type was created, that doesn't mean that a workout room climate like that of India is the best environment for working out. Infrared heat is the same as the heat that radiates from the sun, and it provides for a much lower humidity/drier studio and, therefore, much more accommodating space for workouts.

The same is true for saunas. In a traditional sauna, it is very difficult to breathe at times because the heat is not as radiant as the sun. Rather, it is convection heat, or simply hot air made that way by traditional heaters that heat the room air rather than penetrate your body. The traditional sauna causes you to sweat because the air is hot. Infrared heat causes sweat from external heat and from bodily absorption of infrared radiation.

If you want to try hot exercise, you should always consider the heat source. As stated before, most hot yoga studios simply heat the room with traditional heaters from the HV/AC unit or standard space heaters. It is much more comfortable and beneficial to exercise in infrared heat versus old-school convection-heated air. Why not benefit from the healing and detox properties of infrared while you're working out!? Leave the convection heat behind and opt for infrared when it is available to you.

Chapter 27

HOTWORX® HIIT

HIGH-INTENSITY INTERVAL TRAINING, or HIIT, in normal outdoor climates or in air-conditioned indoor workout environments, when done properly, is an effective addition to any fitness routine. However, when HIIT is combined with infrared energy and heat, the human body responds with a supercharge to its metabolism and with the extra advantage of accelerated detox!

Studies have shown that HIIT training creates significant increases in muscle ability to oxidize fatty acid during exercise. The increasing body of research continues to prove the effectiveness of HIIT for fat burning and weight loss. One such study published in the *Journal of Applied Physiology* recorded data showing that HIIT can increase whole-body fat oxidation by 36 percent.[1]

HIIT requires a burst of high-intensity sets or "intervals" that can shoot the heart rate to 80 percent of max or higher during those intervals. The high-intensity interval bursts are usually accomplished with increased speed from pedaling or rowing, for example, or from

1. Jason L. Talanian, Stuart D. R. Galloway, George J. F. Heigenhauser, Arend Bonen, and Lawrence L. Spriet, "Two Weeks of High-Intensity Aerobic Interval Training Increases the Capacity for Fat Oxidation during Exercise in Women," *Journal of Applied Physiology* 102, no. 4 (April 1, 2007): 1439–47, https://www.physiology.org/doi/full/10.1152/japplphysiol.01098.2006.

increased resistance levels, or from both increased speed combined with increased resistance.

I have consistently worked out at 90–95 percent of my HR max during the HOTWORX® 15-minute HIIT sessions. The infrared heat conditions the body to reach the target HR much faster than traditional weight rooms or fitness studios. Most trainers recommend that clients work hard enough to achieve 80 percent HR max during HIIT sessions. I would recommend that clients try to achieve a range of 75–85 percent of HR max to start before pushing it to higher percentages. By way of definition, the formula for HR max is as follows: take 220 and subtract your age. For example, as of the writing of this chapter, I am 56, so my calculation is 220 – 56 = 164 HR max.

Benefits of HIIT

HIIT is great for weight loss and is generally accepted as more effective for weight loss than traditional cardio or weight training. Logging just a few short HIIT sessions per week can greatly enhance any weight-loss effort. Studies have shown that HIIT improves body composition by decreasing fat mass and increasing lean body mass in both males and females.

HIIT Plus Infrared

Now, let's take HIIT one step further. What about HIIT when combined with an infrared energy and heat environment such as that of the patented three-person, semi-private, HOTWORX® infrared fitness sauna? HOTWORX® introduced this type of workout in February of 2017, and since then, this HIIT form of 3D Training (infrared energy + heat + HIIT) has become wildly popular with studio members.

**No doubt, HIIT creates a more effective workout in less time . . .
but when combined with IR energy and heat, the results compound
to create even more workout efficiency.**

Inside the original HOTWORX® 24 Hour Infrared Fitness Studio in Oxford, Mississippi, the right side of the studio is all HIIT. It consists of a row of saunas dedicated to 15-minute HIIT routines equipped with either Schwinn cycles or Keiser Total Body Trainers. All HOTWORX® studios are equipped with these HIIT saunas.

With perfectly choreographed low-, medium-, and high-tension intervals throughout the 15-minute HIIT workouts, more can be accomplished in less time than ever before. Of course, this is another HOTWORX® original. The bike workout is called Hot Cycle, and the cross-row workout is known as Hot Row. The total-body trainer workout, appropriately named Hot Blast, is unique in that you'll experience a chest press, rowing, and leg press all at once, and what an incredible full-body workout it is in just 15 minutes!

HIIT, especially infrared sauna HIIT, is a calorie scorcher! The research backs this up. "Studies show that 15 minutes of high-intensity interval training burns more calories than jogging on a treadmill for an hour,"[1] reports *Health Fitness Revolution* magazine.

**For those who want to torch the calories quick . . .
go for infrared + HIIT.**

1. "Top 10 Health Benefits of HIIT (High-Intensity Interval Training)," *Health Fitness Revolution*, May 20, 2015, http://www.healthfitnessrevolution.com/top-10-health-benefits-hiit-high-intensity-interval-training/.

Chapter 28

HOTWORX® Innovations

THE ORIGINAL TAGLINE FOR HOTWORX®, which we still use, is "Beyond Hot Yoga." I remember one of our first trade-show expos, where we were showing just the sauna. This was before we introduced the studio franchise. We had that tagline proudly displayed with a poster on the top of the sauna at that fitness industry trade show in Orlando. I will never forget the reaction of one gentleman who happened upon our booth. He noticed the sauna, looked up at the tagline poster, and very slowly said out loud to himself, "Hmm . . . beyond . . . hot . . . yoga"—and stood there, staring at our new method of fitness delivery. At that moment, I felt that we had indeed created something very special for the fitness industry. Since that encounter, we have launched a new fitness franchise built around the whole notion of workouts that go "beyond hot yoga"! I decided to list these workouts in this book. After all, the most important aspect of any exercise is the workout itself.

As a fitness company, we are always looking for ways to improve the workout experience of our customers. We continue to work on new workout types and new exercise sequences and flows. This chapter represents a list of our current hot exercise lineup.

Hot Cycle

We made fitness history again when we introduced HOTWORX®
Hot Cycle. The idea was to offer indoor cycling for clients who wanted to do a quick HIIT session either by itself or in combination for
cross-training with the Hot Yoga or other hot isometric workouts.
Imagine that your workout begins with a 15-minute hot cycle session of pure infrared, then you move straight over to the next HOT-
WORX® sauna for Hot Yoga to round out your day of fitness. We call
this back-to-back cross-training session a Bonfire workout.

Clients use Hot Cycle differently. Some will practice the Bonfire
mentioned above. Others will do a Hot Cycle session after a functional workout for a cardio and lower-body blast finish. Some members
will do multiple back-to-back Hot Cycle sessions. I was working out
at the Oxford, Mississippi, location (the original location) and had a
conversation with a member who told me that she had just finished
her seventh session in a row. Angela is a true HOTWORX® warrior!

Hot Row

While attending a fitness trade show, I noticed a large group of people
doing a very short but super-intense high-intensity interval training
workout on this new machine that was a rower but also a chest press.
I imagined using that machine inside the HOTWORX® sauna and
eventually worked out a plan to install those machines as a part of our
HIIT program in the form of a new workout that we call Hot Row.

Hot Row allows clients to experience a total-body resistance-training HIIT workout in only 15 minutes. The Hot Row workout gives
clients rapid repetitions for rows, chest press, and leg press all at once
inside the HOTWORX® sauna. Customers can experience this incredible total-body resistance and cardio workout while they reap the
benefits of the infrared energy and heat environment.

As of the writing of this book, HOTWORX® is working on a new and even better Hot Row workout, and a patent-pending machine to be announced sometime in 2020.

Hot Blast

The Hot Blast workout was introduced as our most recent HIIT session. It is a unique total-body pounding using the Keiser Total Body Trainer, which is a cardio machine that is a combination indoor cycle and upper-body push-and-pull with right- and left-hand levers. This workout is designed to "blast" the upper body and lower body simultaneously for a 15-minute HIIT routine like no other. This workout allows customers to engage their mind and body for strength, endurance, and high-intensity cardio intervals with this 15-minute infrared session of total-body intensity.

Hot ISO

Hot Iso is the original HOTWORX® workout designed to deliver an awesome sequence of isometric postures borrowing from athletic resistance training and pro-football-style stretching as well as from yoga- and Pilates-style holds. The idea behind the creation of this workout was to maximize the isometric compressions and infrared radiation absorption to create a high level of detox. It is performed for 30 minutes inside the HOTWORX® infrared sauna. There is a modified yoga sun salutation warm-up called the Launch Phase. Following the Launch Phase, clients enter the main workout Flight Phase, which consists of 14 isometric postures beginning with the lower body, then upper body, and finishing with the core. The Landing Phase is the cool-down period ending with a seated, legs-crossed, meditative posture.

Hot Yoga

The HOTWORX® version of hot yoga is certainly more yoga in less time! It is a 30-minute athletic yoga posture sequence, providing clients the most in accelerated infrared yoga results. The idea for HOTWORX® did indeed spring from a notion that people should do yoga in a sauna. Now they can, 24 hours a day.

Hot Pilates

The HOTWORX® version of hot Pilates provides an intense core workout while focusing on the principles of Pilates: centering, concentration, control, precision, breath, and flow. This version of Pilates uses floor exercises within the infrared sauna environment.

Hot Buns

Hot Buns was created for one purpose: to get your BUTT in shape! This intense isometric glute workout is in high demand by HOTWORX® clients. Imagine 30 minutes of nothing but BUTT isometrics—yes, rear-end only inside the infrared sauna. With this session, you work your glutes hard while you sweat out the toxins and absorb the rejuvenating infrared energy.

For those who want a great butt workout to add to their fitness routine, HOT BUNS is rear-end-tensity for real . . .

Hot Barre None

HOTWORX® has become known for its unique workouts, and Hot Barre None is no exception. There is a story about how it came to be.

It was very clear from the beginning that we needed to create a barre workout for HOTWORX®. We knew this early on, but the dilemma was how to mount a ballet barre inside the sauna. We finally identified a manufacturer who made a portable barre that would fit, and we even produced a workout based on the use of that portable barre. We tested the workout for a few months with mostly positive feedback, but it just never seemed to be the right way to deliver a barre workout inside an infrared sauna. The barre itself just seemed to get in the way and reduce the quality of the workout experience. After months of testing and contemplating the marketing of the new workout, it finally dawned on us that by using the back wall of the sauna instead of an actual ballet barre that we just might have the solution. It worked, the workout was incredible, but the problem was, How do you market a barre workout that doesn't use a barre? In a moment of deep marketing thought, it came to me that we should just call the new workout Hot Barre None! We now have a trademark registration on that workout name. It was perfect, and it was very well received when we finally rolled out our barre workout in the fall of 2019.

With the new Hot Barre None session, customers discover muscles that they do not know they have. Using the sauna wall as a workout tool instead of a barre, the virtual instructor guides clients through a half hour of intense postures and slow dynamic reps to help improve poise, posture, strength, and balance. From this workout, customers develop long, lean muscles while they detox from the infrared heat and energy environment.

Hot Warrior

We always have new workout videos that are in development, and out of that pipeline of development came one of our most popular workouts known as Hot Warrior. Hot Warrior is another great HOTWORX® 30-minute isometric workout. We consulted with a pro fitness competitor for insight to help with the choreography and filming of this workout. The idea was to take the Hot ISO, our original HOT-WORX® workout, to a higher level. Mission accomplished!

Everyone has an inner warrior, a power within just waiting to be unleashed. In collaboration, HOTWORX® created a 30-minute infrared fitness routine that draws from yoga, Pilates, and general athletic isometric training methods like the original Hot Iso, but to a "warrior" level. The Hot Warrior is a uniquely choreographed workout and is very challenging. Hot Warrior pushes the fitness envelope and draws from years of training experience to motivate clients to bring their A game.

You will be amazed at the results that can be earned through this hot exercise posture sequence. The multidimensional training method of exercise with infrared energy and heat combined with the more advanced isometric holds accelerates results out of your training time. It accelerates your calorie burn, not to mention the strength gains received from elevated heat shock protein synthesis!

Discover your inner Hot Warrior.

Hot Bands

This is another original 30-minute infrared workout featuring the use of bands for a total-body workout with the combination of isometrics and slow dynamic reps. Hot Bands gives clients the option of a total-body resistance workout inside the infrared sauna. After this session, clients will feel as though they have been through a lightning-fast "hot" weight-training session. In addition to the weight-training type of muscle gains, users of Hot Bands can expect to burn 25–30 percent more calories in 30 minutes compared with Hot Yoga.

Hot Core

Hot Core is the first-ever 30-minute infrared isometric session de-signed for core training and self-myofascial release with the use of a foam roller. The first half of the workout consists of core-focused abdominal, hip, and lower-back work. Core strength is vital. Every-thing begins and ends with the core in fitness and any other full-body movement. The second half of this workout provides for a self-admin-istered deep-tissue massage guided by the virtual instructor. With this HOTWORX® foam-roll routine, there is no better way to accelerate workout recovery and to reduce the appearance of cellulite.

Hot Flex

As of the writing of this book, Hot Flex is in redevelopment as a 30-minute flexibility training session. Originally, this workout was produced as a 15-minute pro-athletics-style infrared stretching rou-tine for use as an advanced warm-up or as an advanced cool down to any of the other HOTWORX® workouts. It could also be used by itself if a member is simply looking to improve flexibility.

The HOTWORX® Bonfire Workout

The practice of adding workout variety through cross-training is gaining in popularity. The reason is that cross-training accelerates performance. The real benefit of cross-training is the gains that come from the blended variety of consistent workout types.

Some people take cross-training to another level by combining different workout types back-to-back during one workout session in a day, as opposed to one workout type per day. It's not for everyone, though. Anyone can do it, but it takes a higher level of motivation.

Everyone should aspire to get to this level. Train your mind. Aspire to achieve something more. Elevate yourself and become a motivated fitness enthusiast to perform this type of training on a consistent weekly basis.

HOTWORX® calls this single-session back-to-back training a Bonfire workout. This workout combines a hot 15-minute HIIT workout—either Hot Cycle, Hot Row, or Hot Blast—then pivots to an isometric sauna for a 30-minute workout of either ISO, yoga, Pilates, or any other you choose to schedule.

The Bonfire usually begins with HIIT for an exhaustive, yet fast, lower-body (Hot Cycle) or total-body (Hot Row or Hot Blast) resistance-training and cardio workout. Once the 15-minute routine is done, customers exit the HIIT sauna and immediately take their shoes and socks off to enter one of the isometric saunas. The 30-minute isometric workout then provides the perfect complement to the HIIT routine. Isometrics such as yoga and Pilates give a great core workout as well as train for balance, flexibility, and detox. Alternatively, if a customer wishes, she can do an isometric workout first, followed immediately by a HIIT session. This incredible workout is an infrared fitness "bonfire"—a must-experience for any aspiring fitness enthusiast.

Isometrics and HIIT are totally different workout types, but they combine to create one great cross-training session. The benefits of isometrics are well documented and include increased circulation, flexibility, and bone and muscle strength gains. High-intensity interval training, as reported by CNN, "encourages your cells to make more proteins to feed their energy-producing machinery—and this arrests the aging process."[1]

This combo can take your infrared training to another level.

1. Susan Scutti, "Interval Training Exercise Could Be a Fountain of Youth," CNN.com, March 8, 2017, http://www.cnn.com/2017/03/07/health/interval-training-exercise-cellular-aging-study/index.html.

HIIT + ISOMETRICS + INFRARED ENERGY AND HEAT = THE BONFIRE WORKOUT!

Virtual Instructors

As an owner of many gyms and fitness facilities throughout my career, I can tell you that one of the most frustrating aspects of gym management is dealing with trainer staff and group fitness instructors. As a certified trainer myself, I have a great deal of respect for the fitness trainers and group instructor professionals, but I am a realist.

What happens when trainers or instructors show up late for a group training session or a group fitness class? Even worse, what happens when they show up unprepared, demotivated, or hungover? What happens is bad customer service. The result is a lower-quality fitness experience for the members and for clients.

Customers deserve better!

HOTWORX® delivers to its members on-time and on-point instruction for every single small-group training session 24 hours a day, every day of the year. This is made possible through the use of virtual instructors. Hours of planning, filming, and editing goes into the creation of every virtually instructed workout. This tireless production is done to ensure that clients receive the best possible fitness experience every time they use a HOTWORX® 24 Hour Infrared Fitness Studio.

Virtual instruction ensures professionalism with every workout!

Virtual instruction ensures that workouts are delivered from experienced and highly skilled trainers and small-group fitness professionals on time, every time! Specially designed software serves up these workouts on time, unbuffered, and to the exact schedule as published by the studio every day of the year 24/7. The advantages of virtual instruction include the following:

- VIs always show up on time.
- VIs are always bringing their A game (no hangovers or low energy).
- VIs are easy to see and to hear within the close proximity of the sauna (and closed-captioned as well for the hearing impaired).
- VIs are certified and experienced.
- Clients can work out with favorite instructors more often.
- Clients can select workouts from a 24/7, 365-days-a-year online schedule.

Hot Foam Rolling

A few years ago, foam rollers began to populate the corners of gym floors all across the globe. A foam roller is simply a tool to allow a user to deliver a self-administered deep-tissue massage. This form of massage is also known as self-myofascial release. Foam rollers come in many sizes, colors, textures, and densities.

As defined by spine-health.com, myofascial release is a "manipulative treatment that attempts to release tension in the fascia due to trauma, posture, or inflammation."[2] With the daily stresses of life and with any rigorous fitness routine, your body will tighten and form trigger points in your muscles and fascia. You can smooth these trig-

---

2. Veritas Health, "Myofascial Release Definition," spine-health.com, accessed May 22, 2020, https://www.spine-health.com/glossary/myofascial-release.

ger points and gain more flexibility by using a foam roller. A consistent practice of foam rolling may also lower your risk of injury.

Fascia is the fibrous tissue that connects all joints, muscles, and organs in the body. There are three types of fascia:

1. Visceral fascia that keeps organs in place
2. Superficial fascia that is found just under the skin
3. Deep fascia that surrounds groups of muscles.

Fascia connects the muscles, nerves, bones, and organs. Foam rolling, which is a deep-tissue massage, provides therapy for the deep fascia. Additionally, hot foam rolling can improve the range of motion of joints where the rolling is applied. One more benefit from hot foam rolling is that you can smooth out the knotted fascia to reduce the appearance of cellulite!

The idea for hot foam rolling for HOTWORX® was inspired by the practice that many athletes now perform with foam rollers for workout recovery. What is good for athletes can usually be incorporated into general fitness routines in a way that beginners and experts alike can appreciate. This is exactly what HOTWORX® intended with the addition of hot foam rolling to the finale of the isometric workouts.

Hot foam rolling provides for a self-administered deep-tissue massage in a unique yet structured format led by a virtual instructor as a part of the cool down after a 30-minute infrared sauna workout. HOTWORX® clients use hot foam rolling to rid their muscles of the tension and knots that restrict movement, cause stress, and impair workout recovery. Of course, with infrared heat, there is even more muscle relaxation as clients work through the myofascial release from the foam rollers.

Foam rolling is way less expensive when compared to the cost of a traditional massage. The average price for a deep-tissue massage (as of the publishing of this book) is around $110 to $120 per session at your typical day spa. Why pay for that when you can achieve the same result with a foam roller at the end of your workout?

I will personally swear by the practice of foam rolling. It really can be a full-body self-administered deep-tissue massage and produces the same results that can be obtained from a professional massage therapist.

HOTWORX® isometric workouts incorporate foam rolling at the end of the infrared workout session. Foam rolling combined with infrared is an extremely effective method for acceleration of workout recovery! Don't leave the studio or gym without getting your roll on!

Yoga Mat (and Towel) for Hot Isometrics

Your yoga mat and towel are personal things. These two items are as important to an isometric workout as a good pair of shoes are to a runner. When people experience yoga, Pilates, and other forms of isometrics with a really good mat and towel, they will never go back to a lesser-quality experience.

I have taken yoga from many places and have used and/or rented the house mats and towels on many occasions. I have to say that some of the larger fitness chains that offer yoga pay no attention to the quality of their mats and towels. At one international yoga chain, the towel that I rented looked like a small bath towel from a roadside motel, and that is exactly how it performed for me during that yoga session. Usually, the mats are too small, and the towels never fit right over the mat.

With HOTWORX®, we set out to create the perfect mat and towel for hot isometrics, and I do believe that we succeeded because our customers love them.

Before we rolled out the first HOTWORX® infrared workout sauna, we had no idea how popular our mats and towels would be. Now we manufacture them by the thousands per month. We knew that we were making them out of high-quality materials, but we didn't foresee how many people would want a mat and towel of their own instead of renting them. We were just determined to make a great yoga mat and yoga towel, and that we did.

Why are our mats and towels so loved by clients? Quite simply, they work well! The size of the towel is a perfect match for the size of the mat. The materials used in manufacturing provide for a very high-quality experience, and both the mat and towel last a very long time. In fact, I have yet to see a mat or towel that had to be replaced even after daily usage over and over and constant washing of the towels. The towels are made of eco-friendly and super-absorbent microfiber material with silica gel particles on the reverse side to eliminate slipping. The HOTWORX® mat is infused with all-natural hemp fibers that are ideal for HOTWORX® and any other floor-exercise programs or routines. The honeycomb design of the mat padding provides for superior footing while practicing yoga, Pilates, and other forms of isometrics. Quality makes the difference when it comes to mats and towels.

The best way I can describe this love for our yoga mats and towels is to liken it to a good pair of ski boots and skis. As an avid snow skier, I know that the perfect pair of skis and boots make a huge difference in performance. The same is true for workout performance when you use high-quality gear! Yoga enthusiasts want an increased level of performance with an optimum workout mat and towel. The bottom line is that everyone wants the very best workout that they can obtain, for sure! The right mat and towel can give you that ninja-like edge for yoga and other isometrics.

Chapter 29

HOTWORX® Zero Impact

ONE OF THE GREATEST ADVANTAGES of yoga and other isometric types of workouts are the health benefits without the bodily wear and tear of high-impact movement. Indoor cycling and rowing provide solid low-to-zero-impact workouts, too. Infrared heat makes low-impact training even more attractive because of the workout recovery component that it adds to the fitness equation.

Pro-athlete-style fitness training is all the rage these days. As a former athlete, I can attest to the effectiveness of ballistic movement and plyometrics, but injuries are sure to occur with such high-impact methods. While plyometrics can provide excellent training for sports, there is a high probability of risk for injury, and I would not recommend it for general fitness programs.

Recently, I was speaking to another fitness professional who made the prediction that soon, there would be a wave of long-term injuries caused by excessive plyometric exercise practiced for general fitness reasons. Unfortunately, I believe that he is right.

Flawed plyometric programming and large fitness-training classes are contributing to the problem. Plyometrics, or "jump training," can be very dangerous, mainly because of the stress from the landings. The high acceleration and landing impact can result in wear and tear to the spine and joints. The damage can be cumulative and can result in long-term injury over time.

Reports have shown that high-impact repetitive exercise results in spinal shrinkage. Three or more times your body weight that occurs upon landing from a plyometric jump, when performed repeatedly over time can cause irreparable damage.

Injuries occur when tissues are forced to adapt to situations that require more work than the tissues can structurally tolerate. High-impact exercises often cause injuries because of this very reason.

Fortunately, there are better ways to achieve optimum levels of fitness. Zero-impact programs can easily get your heart rate to the right level quickly, especially when they are performed in a heated studio. HOTWORX® provides a variety of infrared workouts that are all designed for zero-impact fitness. With our 3D Training Method that combines zero-impact exercise with heat and infrared energy, the metabolism is accelerated, and the time to warm up to the full workout intensity is reduced to provide for more fitness results in less time with no impact to the joints!

Principle of Progressive Overload

This principle is fundamental to fitness. It is, perhaps, the most foundational component. The whole idea of a fitness program is to enable a client to see positive results. To see results, one has to progress to higher levels of accomplishment. In other words, the level of workout intensity should remain high for each workout so that the effect of training is greater as time goes forward. One way to keep intensity high is to overload your muscles, including the heart, with higher levels of physical stress in the effort to make gains. When your body adapts to a heavier weight or a longer stretch, then it is time to overload again to reach the appropriate level of intensity and challenge as loop of progression continues.

As you progress, don't fall into the popular trap of changing the workout (within a workout type) every time. Constant changing within a workout type causes chaos with respect to measurability. Carefully consider your level of intensity and your level of awareness as you step up your game. Attempt to perfect your workout with progressive overload for specific postures or with specific exercises as a way to know how much better you are performing each time you train.

Try a routine of consistent isometrics with a solid sequence of postures for at least one full 90-day run before changing the exercises. You will see the gains through easy measurement and increased mind/body connection. Connect with your body mentally and take it through flexibility, balance, and endurance transformation. HOTWORX® can provide you with this type of routine, and you can experience it all inside an infrared energy and heat environment.

I believe that a workout routine should be revised sensibly, meaning incrementally. I have found through experience that a biannual basis is most effective. We revise our workout videos on a biannual basis for HOTWORX®, and we stick to the fundamental postures that are necessary for our clients to measure their progress, such as wall sits, isometric squats, and planks. Incremental adaptation to sensible routine change is the best way forward to achieve steady and continual progress.

Focus on how high you can take your intensity level for each exercise first before changing the exercise. There is no need to confuse yourself because your muscles will not be confused either way. Muscles respond to stimuli, period.

If You Need to Take a Break

As I described earlier in the book, at one point, I was forced by my doctor to stop training entirely for a month because of minor surgery. I did have time to think about how I would manage this time off from training, and I decided to train with super intensity up until the day before the surgery. I maintained my weight-training regimen and my HOTWORX® infrared workout sessions, but I did incorporate higher levels of intensity before surgery.

I have been active in fitness and athletic training for more than 30 years now. Looking back on times in my past when I took breaks from training for reasons such as injuries or rest after major competitions, I always noticed significant decreases in strength and conditioning. To my astonishment, this time, I actually felt like I picked up right where I left off even after 30 days of inactivity! I noticed it, and all the people with whom I work out noticed it and made comments.

What was the X factor? The obvious difference for me this time around was the HOTWORX® 3D Training.

You should always eat clean food and keep up sufficient levels of protein on a forced break, just like you do when you are in training, but think about the quality of your fitness routine before a planned break from training as well. I am proof that the quality of training matters when you are forced into a break. In my case, adding infrared energy and heat to my workout was just as important as clean eating. A quality workout infused with infrared and heat can enhance and prolong your level of fitness, enabling you to ride out a break from activity.

Chapter 30

High Profile HOTWORX Users

CELEBRITIES AND PRO ATHLETES have used and continue to use the HOTWORX® workouts and 3D Training Method. Early on in the initial marketing phase of HOTWORX®, we were fortunate to install one of our saunas at the residence of actress and comedian Jenny McCarthy and her husband, Donnie Wahlberg. After we installed her unit, Jenny posted on social media about HOTWORX®: "I knew my fitness prayers had been answered."

Since that time, reality show stars and professional athletes from many different sports have discovered the fitness benefits of HOTWORX®.

As a former NPC National Collegiate Bodybuilding Champion, I can tell you that paying attention to every training routine detail makes the difference between winning and losing a title. Then, beyond an athletic career, I promise you that details still matter. Paying attention to how you train for fitness can have a huge impact on your quality of life. Recently, I have been listening to stories from athletes and former athletes who have used HOTWORX® infrared workouts to enhance their competition training routines and their post-career fitness activities. One such story really grabbed my attention last summer.

Pat McAfee, former NFL punter for the Indianapolis Colts turned football and professional wrestling analyst, has a very entertaining video podcast, *The Pat McAfee Show.* I recommend it to anyone who enjoys a raw and funny take on sports. One day at my office, I over-heard people talking about the Pat McAfee podcast, and they were discussing how he was talking about HOTWORX® on his show. Apparently, his girlfriend had become a member of the franchise location in Indianapolis, and he was working out with her at that studio.

On this particular podcast, he spent about 12 minutes talking specifically about his experience at HOTWORX® with his girlfriend.

The Pat McAfee Show is a great video podcast. It's definitely worth subscribing to his youtube channel, and if you want to watch the show where he mentions HOTWORX®, you can go to https://www.youtube.com/watch?v=WMKPbiBFelg.

Jeremy Fikac, former Major League Baseball relief pitcher for the San Diego Padres, Oakland A's, and Montreal Expos saw the benefits of HOTWORX® and made the decision to become a franchise owner with his partner, Jason Scott, in the Austin, Texas market area.

Jeremy has this to say about HOTWORX®:

"The concepts behind HOTWORX® 3D training allows for anyone, no matter their background of fitness, to benefit and impact their overall health in a dynamic way. As a franchise owner I have seen positive outcomes from members in ways such as weight loss, flexibility, and most importantly confidence in their selfs! HOTWORX® is an innovative and fresh fitness concept that everyone can benefit from!"

PART V

Starting Your Own HOTWORX® Studio

"It is much better to stand out than to blend in."

Chapter 31

What Makes HOTWORX® Special?

THE SIMPLE ANSWER IS we focus on more results in less time for our customers. The more complex answer lies in the details of what it takes to deliver fast fitness results through innovative technology.

When an individual begins to think about opening a business, the first thing she should consider is how to differentiate the store from other brands in the chosen industry. This is where HOTWORX® shines. As the first-ever 24/7 infrared fitness-training center, it is easy for customers to see the difference in the vast ocean of health clubs selling memberships to the public these days.

The uniqueness of the brand is why HOTWORX® continues to grow at a very rapid pace. With more than 500 new HOTWORX® studio franchises now either open or in development from coast to coast across the USA—a feat accomplished in just three years leading up to the date of this book publishing—the company is poised to bring the franchise concept to every fitness-minded neighborhood in the country, and across the world. HOTWORX® allows customers to experience a new and better way to get healthy and to stay in shape through hot exercise technology.

Let's face it, we want convenience so we can obtain desired results without wasting time. As a businessperson, I am not really big on long, philosophical mission statements. Rather, I prefer to let the business do the talking by providing a great product and a great service. That being said, after a few short weeks of the opening of the original location in Oxford, Mississippi, we realized that our de facto mission was simply to provide great workouts fast so that people could have more time to live. Thus, our slogan (or mission statement, if you rather) became "More Workout, Less Time."

In fitness, one way to know how successful a gym operates is to measure the repeat usage of the facility by its customers. HOT-WORX® has an incredible repeat-usage rate. For typical gyms, daily usage hovers around 10–15 percent of the total membership base per day. With HOTWORX®, the usage is MUCH higher, reaching more than 30 percent at times. Customers want more from their workouts, and in less time. Getting better workouts and saving time will never go out of style! Technology has paved the way for this new infrared fitness reality, and HOTWORX® believes in this bold fitness frontier.

Business Firsts

I would argue that the most important component of business marketing is uniqueness. Of course, there are many important aspects of marketing, such as professional imagery and ad production. Still, if the product is not memorable based on its uniqueness, then it will fail to gain sizable traction in the marketplace. Market differentiation happens when there are product and service uniquenesses.

The market differentiation that the HOTWORX® franchise brings to the table has many layers, not just the 24/7 infrared workouts. There are many "firsts" in terms of fitness technology that HOT-WORX® has introduced to the industry. These include the now patented 63-square-foot, three-person infrared workout sauna; virtual instruction for small-group infrared training; the "silent" functional trainer; the Burn Off App; the 30-minute infrared isometric workout; and the 15-minute infrared HIIT, to name a few.

As I write this book, we are in the midst of the development of our new virtual personal trainer (VPT) program to enhance the functional training area of the studio known as the FX Zone. The VPT program allows customers who have an upgraded membership to create a tailored, virtually instructed, functional training routine to enable them with more tools to achieve their fitness goals as a complement to their infrared training routine. This new technology will become available at all HOTWORX® locations in 2020, probably around the time of this book publishing.

Perhaps the most important HOTWORX® differentiator, though, is the 24-hour availability of hot yoga (along with other, more inventive hot exercise options). With the HOTWORX® infrared workout sauna, our members utilize access to a variety of hot exercise options 24 hours a day. This is a huge first mover, a market advantage for our franchise owners and especially for our customers. In the modern world, traditional fitness studio class schedules are just not convenient for everyone. Even for those who maintain a normal daily work schedule, they often prefer to work out late at night, super early in the morning, or at odd hours during the weekend. Hot exercise becoming available 24/7 is a game-changing difference.

Another way to achieve market differentiation is to open a boutique business. Boutique businesses are known for their uniqueness, and boutiques of all types are gaining popularity the world over. Generally, we understand a boutique to be a small, exclusive business that offers a very specialized form of services or products. What began as a term to describe a small clothing store now gives definition to many other business types such as hotels, advertising agencies, and health clubs.

HOTWORX® differentiates itself as a boutique fitness center as well. HOTWORX® is a unique fitness boutique, though!

Clients want a "specialty" experience from boutique studios that focus on quality over size. Fitness members also want multiple workout options. There are very few boutique fitness studios that can offer more than one workout type. Typically they will offer one or two workout types such as yoga, Pilates, or indoor cycling. HOTWORX® is unique not only as a boutique but as a boutique with over 10 different workout session types to choose from.

HOTWORX® 24 Hour Infrared Fitness Studios are boutiques that specialize in small-group infrared training. Still, the market difference is that there are a variety of workouts and hot exercise options way beyond what is offered at the usual studio. HOTWORX® provides the best of both worlds, a boutique atmosphere and the workout variety of a much larger multi-service fitness facility.

If you are an entrepreneur, or aspire to be one, you should always strive for market differentiation. As you make the effort to be unique, don't copy, be unique, be real, and be first!

Fitness Instruction

In an article written by Grace DeSimone, editor of the American College of Sports Medicine's Resources for the Group Exercise Instructor, she makes the point that boutique fitness studios have created communities of like-minded people and bonded them together "through activity." She adds that technology and more athleticism has attracted a new breed of instructor that she calls a "hybrid trainer."[1]Indeed, the fitness instructor has evolved. Many boutique fitness studios are now finding ways to utilize virtual instructors and virtual trainers. This is certainly the way to ensure that clients always receive quality instruction. The HOTWORX® franchise pioneered the use of virtual instructors 24/7 inside an infrared sauna and uses its patented three-person saunas that are lined up side by side in rows inside the studio workout area.

There's no doubt that boutiques have elevated the coolness factor in fitness.

No Wasted Space

We created the HOTWORX® heated infrared exercise system for business owners to improve their bottom line by improving the waistlines of their customers. HOTWORX® is a workout system based on "hot exercise," a term that we coined. We use a patented infrared sauna

1. Grace DeSimone, www.acsm.org, Nov 20, 2017, https://www.acsm.org/blog-detail/acsm-certified-blog/2017/11/20/boutique-fitness-studios-reviving-group-exercise-trend.

system to service three clients at a time for their isometric and HIIT workout needs.

As an entrepreneur who has owned gyms and spas since the 1980s, I can certainly appreciate good use of space to generate income. In fact, I would argue that income per square foot is the most important metric for a brick-and-mortar business, second only to bottom-line profit. We invented the HOTWORX® sauna and suite of hot workouts to bring "cha-ching" to an entrepreneur's cash register (or POS system, as it is known these days) from a very small amount of square footage. Only 63sq ft is needed per HOTWORX® sauna, and that small space provides for a constant stream of small-group training sessions back-to-back, automated, and on a 24/7, 365-day-per-year basis!

Entrepreneurs should focus on income per square foot because every square inch must be accounted for and contribute to the success of your business! Is that real estate contributing to positive results for your members and clients? I am a firm believer in NO WASTED SPACE! At HOTWORX®, we don't have any space wasted on an office. All business is conducted behind the counter and in a way that creates an opportunity for staff to mingle and to have more face time with customers. Technology has erased the need for an office.

I designed the original location to utilize every square inch to the maximum profit potential. Everything in the floor plan matters, from the placement of the front counter to the location of the vending machine to the bathrooms, lockers, and the point where the battle rope is installed. Customer traffic flow and placement of functional equipment to mirror proximity are extremely important. The typical 2,300-sq-ft, 10-sauna HOTWORX® layout provides for an incredible amount of daily workout capacity with approximately 1,600 individual workout slots on the schedule in each 24-hour day. Workout capacity is crucial, and everything has to make for a super-efficient use of leased space. Every detail matters in business.

No Wasted Time

Time is just as important as space to a brick-and-mortar business owner, especially a fitness business owner. Make every effort to maximize space and time with your business. Space + exercise capacity + time = results to the bottom line in the business of fitness.

It just makes good sense to provide the perfect 30-minute workout. As a fitness business owner, why not try 30 minutes instead of 60, or 90 if you can achieve the same level of customer satisfaction? It's a win-win solution so long as the customer is obtaining the results they are looking for.

Why should a customer have to spend 60 or 90 minutes of her life working out when she can reap the same, or even more, benefits in 30 minutes? I have experienced packed hot yoga studios, with 50 people squeezed into a room for 90 minutes, and it is not a good time. After a few of those sessions, I began to think, "Why do I have to do this to get the workout I want? There has to be a faster way to get the results and to have a better workout experience!" Many of us simply do not have the luxury of more time and, even if we did, we want a better fitness experience for sure.

This is why I knew that the HOTWORX® routine had to be based on a 30-minute workout. Given the right studio climate and the proper level of intensity, 30 minutes is the perfect amount of time for a workout. The type of heat is supremely important, too. Infrared heat is by far the best for workouts. Far infrared heat at 125°F is ideal when combined with isometrics for the perfect 30-minute workout.

Save time! Don't waste it with 60- and 90-minute workouts if you can offer the perfect 30-minute workout for your clients! If you want to be a part of this new infrared fitness frontier, you should consider opening a HOTWORX® franchise.

Give serious consideration to how you manage workout time for your clients and members. Give them good technology and the most results possible for the time they spend in your fitness facility. Your bottom line will thank you.

What Our Customers Say

As I have traveled coast to coast visiting HOTWORX® franchises, one thing that I hear from the customers at all the locations is how the 3D workouts have elevated their quality of life. I have heard this from mom/daughter teams and individuals who are yoga instructors, celebrities, professional athletes, doctors, fitness competitors, police officers, firefighters, and nurses. No matter what the physical goal is, from an athlete to a working mom or a homemaker, this revolutionary new workout program delivers the desired results.

From a business standpoint, there is no better advertising for a fitness studio than that of user-generated, unsolicited online content. Customers use social media and other web portals to spread the word about the benefits of hot exercise. Here are a few examples in their own words:

> *Five-star Yelp rating from a customer in San Antonio, Texas:*
>
> OMG, this is beyond amazing!!!! Genius!!! Like nothing I've ever tried!!! I love to work out, have always done tennis, boot camps, etc. but had to give them all up because I've had serious back, hip, and leg pain several years now have tried so mango [sic] different exercises, therapies, etc. . . . I started yoga for stretching, etc, and liked it but hard to schedule, and pretty expensive . . . and my schedule is too erratic for a regular gym. . . . This I can schedule with an app the day of, and if I get delayed, I just cancel it and add the next [session]. . . . So convenient for me! The reason I LOVE this concept is that my joint pain and

muscle pain has gone to almost nothing!!! The calorie burn for a short workout (plus the crazy afterburner) is awesome!!! My skin has completely changed, it's tighter, less fine lines, I walk out of my HWX session a sweaty mess, but I feel 15 years younger! I try to do a HIIT workout first. I prefer the [cycle session], only 15 minutes, but it amps up my calorie burn. I've been doing an isometric [session] immediately following, either yoga, ISO, or core usually since my schedule is so erratic, I sometimes try something new because I can just schedule it with my app when I'm available... By doing the HIIT first, I start sweating and feeling the intensity as soon as I start the yoga. . . . I used to not be able to do a child's pose, and by the end of the session, I am deep into that stretch. . . . The infrared keeps me from getting sore, and I feel the effects for a couple of days after a workout. If I do a personal trainer session anywhere else where I have to do multiple wall squats, lunges, & planks, I can't sit down properly for a week. . . . Because of the infrared, I do the ISO or Warrior [session], which is virtually like having a serious personal trainer kick your butt . . . and the infrared eliminates the soreness completely. . . . Of course, you have to drink tons of water . . . but for sure, if you have any muscle or joint pain and other exercise has been difficult for you, try this!!!! You will feel like younger self!!! I've had people ask me what kind of facials I'm doing because my skin looks so great. . . . So that's an added bonus!!! Again. . . . This is GENIUS!!!

Instagram post from a customer in Gainesville, Florida:

[My friend] and I decided to step out of our comfort zone and try a hot-yoga style [session] with HOTWORX® Gainesville. We were AMAZED!!! With private saunas/workout rooms, you get to choose an exercise of your liking and be led by a virtual instructor through an intense session of torching calories. Of the variety they provided, we decided to try the warrior [session] and tested our abilities through isometric, yoga, and Pilates movements. For two gals that lift weights consistently, the 30-minutes session left us SHAKING! If you wanna try it out for yourself, get on their website and get that FREE trial (feel free to mention my name!) and challenge your body to its core!

Instagram post from a customer, location unknown:

After graduating from college, working out consistently was a major STRUGGLE. I would go to the gym, run a mile, and then all motivation was out the window. I joined Orange Theory and had been doing it since 2015. I loved it for a while, but it broke the bank, and I eventually stopped seeing results. I recently tried HOTWORX®, and I AM LITERALLY OBSESSED. I'm not kidding, y'all, I left and went straight to Orange Theory to cancel my membership (sorry Orange Theory peeps). HOTWORX® is a virtually instructed exercise program with infrared sauna rooms. You can do 30-minute isometric workouts or 15-min. HIIT sessions. It takes a lot to make me sweat when working out, and I leave HOTWORX® completely drenched after just 15 mins! I'm not going to lie, I don't LOVE working out . . . I mean, it's fine, but I would much rather be on a patio eating a cheese board. I wish I could say I was like [my DJ friend] and worked out to improve my health, but I'm just trying not to get a dad bod before he does. LAST PART OF THIS RAND: I BURNED MORE CALORIES IN 30 mins THAN I DID IN AN HOUR AT ORANGE THEORY! Side note: this is not an ad for HOTWORX® . . . they don't even know my name.

HOTWORX® franchise owners throughout the USA and other parts of the world are growing their businesses through online (and offline) word-of-mouth hot exercise buzz.

Trend, Not a Fad

I hear of people who complain about that "thing" that has grown to incredible heights and has been around for a long time and how they should have bought stock in it years ago, or that they should have purchased the franchise before the territory was sold out. The fact is, those voices failed to recognize the difference between a fad and a trend and did not act on the investment opportunity accordingly.

A fad is a temporary fashion, but a trend is a sustained movement. Hot yoga has been around now for half a century. I dare say that nobody considers it to be a fad anymore.

What turns into a trend for the long term is spawned from discoveries of how to make something good even better. Of course, our example would be yoga. Yoga has been around for many centuries. The creation of hot yoga in the 1960s made yoga better. Then, in 2014, the innovation of the HOTWORX® infrared sauna went beyond hot yoga to not only improve yoga but to make other isometric and HIIT workout forms even better!

Using infrared for fitness is an idea that is changing the way that people work out and is beginning to make a serious statement throughout the industry, too, in the same way that suspension training and workout resistance bands did when they were introduced. As a testament to this, the HOTWORX® franchise concept grew at a faster rate during its first 18 months than other well-known 1,000-plus-location fitness concepts did in their first 18 months. To create a movement, make something that is already good even better!

One reason for the growth of the franchise is the patented HOTWORX® sauna. It creates a superior hot exercise environment for a small group to enjoy (small-group training is another trend that wasn't a fad). The sauna is inexpensive to set up and only requires a small amount of real estate. As I alluded to earlier, this mini-studio yields a very high revenue return for only 63sq ft of space.

Infrared is a market mover and a fitness industry game-changer. It represents a new frontier of fitness. HOTWORX® is blazing the trail as the infrared fitness pioneer!

Look outside of our industry. Take phones, for example. Obviously, the telephone was an invention that is still "trending" today. The telephone has been around for more than a century now, but there have been many upgrades and innovations applied to it over the years. Nobody uses a rotary phone anymore. Push-button phones were introduced by the Bell Telephone Company in 1963, leading everyone into a better way to dial. You may be surprised to know that the first car phones were put into service in 1946, representing a telephone game change that would take off in the '80s.

Apple completely reinvented the phone again with the introduction of the iPhone in the summer of 2007. Five years after that, Apple became the most valuable company in the world. Apple has remained one of the most valuable companies in the world for quite some time and in August of 2019, reclaimed the title once again. The iPhone was not a fad—it was a distillation of discoveries turned into an invention that made a long-term trend even better, and it continues to evolve and improve.

How Can I Recognize a Fad?

The best way to describe a fad is to say that it is a temporary fashion . . . a flash in the pan. The fitness landscape is littered with the carcasses of products and brands that were fads. Take a look back. Do you remember the Ab-Buster, Bowflex, ThighMaster, stripper pole aerobics? All were flash-in-the-pan offerings that failed to remain relevant in the arc of the general fitness trend. And, I have to say, there is the one product that really gets under my skin as a fitness professional, the modified dumbbell Shake Weight. Remember that one? What an exercise folly and a fad for the record books if there ever was one.

Now, what about fitness products that have withstood the test of time? The Reebok Step is such a great example. Step workouts are still alive and well! I also have to recognize the TRX brand and suspension training as one of those inventions that became a long-term trend. As a TRX certified trainer, I can tell you that suspension training is an awesome, zero-impact addition to any functional workout. I believe that infrared fitness training is another movement like TRX and the Reebok Step that is based on a trend that will be around forever in some form.

Customers want more from their workouts, and in less time. The infrared trend delivers more workout in less time, and getting better workouts and saving time will never go out of style!

Making Money with a HOTWORX® Franchise

One of the best ways to understand whether a particular franchise is the right investment for you is to find out who is buying and take a look at some of their results in terms of profit.

Here's the story of my franchise location. In the fall of 2016, I decided to open the first-ever 24-hour infrared fitness studio. As I was contemplating where to open this concept studio, one of my best friends from college told me that I should open in Oxford, Mississippi. On February 24, 2017, I published this blog post to HOTWORX®. net:

Come See the Future of Fitness . . . You're Invited!

Now Open . . .
The first-ever 24 Hour Infrared Fitness Studio franchise!!!

I have been keeping this one on the DL for several weeks. It's time to let everyone know now, though. We have been quietly working behind the scenes in Oxford, MS (home of Ole Miss) to bring to life the first-ever 24 Hour Infrared Fitness Studio, and now it is open and flush with happy members! They are all "sweaty and smiling" from the workout experience at the first of many more HOTWORX® 24 Hour Infrared Fitness Studios to come. We have investors and prospective franchisees now lined up to get involved. You might want to consider reserving a territory soon!

I know it's taboo to turn a blog post into a sales pitch, but I just can't help myself today.

Big shout-out to my partner in the Oxford location, and college best friend from way back, John Antwine. As any fellow Ole Miss graduate should, he originally pushed for Oxford as the first location. We also have investor partners that helped make the project possible, huge thanks to two business professionals and great guys from Jackson, MS, John Thomas, and Rett Crowder.

From idea last November to opening in February, it took only 12 weeks to get there, and that, my friends, is fast to open a brick-and-mortar business concept from scratch! Consider that we negotiated and signed a long-term lease, and we began with an old building (formally the Oxford Eagle Newspaper). We then took that raw space, gutted it, and immediately began construction on the historical square in Oxford. We crossed every hurdle to get there, including all of the necessary permits, the historical committee (two formal city meetings with them), ADA, and the fire marshal. We created all of the things that are needed to launch a new franchise, including the legal documentation.

Whew! It has been a whirlwind, but it is all worthwhile when you see the satisfaction on the faces of our customers.

Of course, none of this could have been possible so quickly without the support, dedication, and focus of our HOTWORX® corporate team in Marrero, LA. GREAT JOB, GUYS!!!

Stay tuned for massive location growth and billions of calories and fat cells burned in the process!!!

Earn the Burn!

There was a clause in our original HOTWORX® partnership agreement for Oxford that called for an increase in ownership for John Antwine from 10 percent to 24.5 percent so long as we hit 300 members before the end of October 2017. We surpassed the 300 mark on March 23, 2017, only five weeks after opening for business. Needless to say, the partners and I were ecstatic to see such rapid membership sales results.

I am very proud of our first full fiscal year (January to December 2018) at the original HOTWORX® location in Oxford. Here were the results:

The 2018 total revenue came in at $604,594, with an after-tax profit of $286,367.

Full fiscal year number one for our first true franchise locations had good outcomes as well. The first four true franchise locations (locations not owned by me or corporate) opened with four separate owner groups from three different states. The Flower Mound, Texas, location opened September 14, 2017, and its 2018 financial results were $474,284 in revenue, with an after-tax profit of $209,262. Madison, Mississippi, opened that same day and, in 2018, posted revenues of $441,106, with after-tax profits of $90,769. The third true franchise opened for business November 20, 2017, in Enid, a small town in northern Oklahoma. Despite the small-town demographics, Enid still delivered a solid first-year performance with $256,044 in revenues and an after-tax profit of $82,724.

True franchise number four opened in Lubbock, Texas, on January 23, 2018. Please note that the first-year results for this location had only eight days' worth of revenues in the first month due to opening for business in late January. Despite a partial first month, Lubbock did not disappoint. This franchise posted a first-year revenue figure of $523,741 and a profit after tax of $280,762.

That is a pretty darn good return on investment for the first full year of operations. The total investment for a location then was approximately $350,000.

We continue to see first-year results like these posted throughout the country in many states. I always tell people that a focus on long-term profit is the most important metric to obsess over. I go on to tell them that if you follow the franchise system with a maniacal intent on delivering great infrared workouts to your customers, they will reward you with great profits, and your clients will be happy for you, so long as you continue to give them more value than they bargained for! No matter the product, but especially in fitness, customer experience and results will always reign supreme. Profit is a measure of how well you take care of your customers, and this should be a long-term investment. It's hard work to deliver great service day in and day out, but never forget, in all things, you get out what you put in!

Most of our franchise owners start out as customers. They join a HOTWORX® studio, and then, based on the passion they gain from their fitness experience and physical results, they will seek to open their own location.

Bobby Petrino, the acclaimed college and NFL head football coach, and a member of the Orlando HOTWORX®, was a customer who had one of the best workouts of his life at that location. He wanted to open a business with his son in Denver and chose to open a HOTWORX® franchise. In a *USA Today* article, Coach Petrino was asked about his plans in the interim while he prepares to coach again. "He said he and his son are opening a couple of HOTWORX® infrared fitness studios in Colorado."[1]. At the time of the writing of this book, Coach Petrino's son, Bobby, is well into the development of their first location in Colorado.

His son had this to say about the decision to open HOTWORX® franchises.

1. Steve Brawner, "Bobby Petrino Says He Wants to Coach Again, Apologizes for Arkansas Scandal," *USA Today*, September 10, 2019, https://www.usatoday.com/story/sports/ncaaf/2019/09/10/bobby-petrino-wants-to-coach-apologizes-for-scandal/2272439001/.

For years now, we have looked into the idea of buying into a franchise. However, nothing had sparked our interest at the time. When we discovered HOTWORX® in 2018 and the benefits it offered to people, we were immediately interested. HOTWORX® is not a traditional fitness studio. HOTWORX® is the only fitness studio in the world that can offer its clients the ability to work out while recovering and detoxing the body. With the innovation of HOTWORX®'s method of 3D Training—heat, infrared energy, and exercise—we can have an impact on someone's life that far outreaches a good physique or muscle tone. A franchised business offers us the independence of owning our own business with an already established and successful business system. We couldn't be happier with our decision to invest in HOTWORX® and to start significantly changing lives![2]

2. Stephen Smith, "The Best Workout, Recovery, and Detox," HOTWORX®.net, September 16, 2019, https://hotworx.net/news/the-best-workout-recovery-and-detox/.

Conclusion

SOON AFTER WE ROLLED the first HOTWORX® sauna off the assembly line and onto the floor of the International Franchise Expo in New York City in 2015, I knew from the reactions of expo attendees, and from personal use, that the workouts were very different, in a good way. The HOTWORX® infrared sauna workout was far superior to those heated yoga sessions that had served as an inspiration to me in the past. It was evident that beyond just the heat of the infrared sauna, there was something more. It had to do with the way that the air felt on my body—dry, comfortable heat—and the deep penetration of the lightwave energy inside my body. It was different, a workout in a room like none other. It was clear to me that this was a new workout dimension yet to be codified.

With the advent of this new workout environment, I reflected on my past training experience, and it dawned on me that I had evolved my workouts through the years in a simple 1-2-3 progression. First, there were weight-training and cardio exercises that were performed primarily inside an air-conditioned gym. Then came hot yoga. For me, this was Bikram yoga, which I added to my fitness program in 2014—my first foray into an indoor heated fitness workout environment. Bikram, and most hot yoga studios, still use convection heating, which is usually an HV/AC system whereby the hot air is blown in through vents. Some of these studios simply use space heaters that are plugged into the wall. My third phase of personal workout evolution came with our development of the HOTWORX® workout method, which incorporates the use of heat and infrared energy combined with isometrics and HIIT. We know this as 3D Training now.

This 1-2-3 workout evolution, in my mind, was like art, advancing from a one-dimensional pencil drawing to a two-dimensional color painting and finally to three-dimensional sculpture. Or, imagine watching a film in black and white, then seeing it in color and finally watching it again in full-color 3D.

This art analogy is where the term 3D Training came from and is what we now use to reference our training method. The HOTWORX® 3D Training Method has transformed my body and my life. In many ways, I feel like I did in my 20s. My brain is energized and focused. My body is more durable, flexible, and strong from this infrared method of fitness. The isometrics and HIIT training combined with the heat and the infrared lightwave energy has to be experienced by every human on this planet!

Thus, we have launched HOTWORX® as a franchise so that we can bring it to people all over the world to touch their lives with positive energy and to give them a better way to achieve a higher quality of life, as well as to better equip our customers to win in the race to be human on their own terms.

As a former athlete, I can tell you that what it takes to be a winner in sports is very similar to what it takes to win in business and in personal fitness programs. Words like "dream," "discipline," and "dedication" come to mind. For example, what began with a dream to provide the very best workouts for people who have limited time to train has now become the fastest-growing franchise in the fitness business.

The uniqueness of a product is important for sure. Still, for any "dream" or vision to have a fighting chance for success, it has to be supported by an absolute dedication to a set of goals and must practice the necessary "discipline" to see it all the way through!

With HOTWORX®, we set out from day one to open 500 locations in the first five years of operations. I am happy to announce, as of the date of publishing of this book, that we are on track to achieve that goal. We opened the very first location for HOTWORX® on February 13, 2017. Now, after three years, there are more than 150 locations opened, and another 500-plus are in various stages of development. The dream is now within reach!

Another great boutique fitness brand, Anytime Fitness, achieved 977 locations after seven years of franchising.[1]

We believe firmly that we, too, can achieve and even go beyond what other great fitness brands have accomplished.

For any winning program, whether it be a sports team, a business, or a personal fitness regime, to sustain performance at a high level, it can never lose sight of what got it there.

For HOTWORX®, our purpose since the beginning, now, and for every year to come is to deliver great workouts in less time through 24/7 access to infrared training for our customers.

The future of fitness is HOT EXERCISE.

1. "Anytime Fitness," *Entrepreneur*, updated January 2, 2020, https://www.entrepreneur.com/franchises/anytimefitness/306988.

About the Author

STEPHEN P. SMITH is the Founder of Planet Beach and HOT-WORX®. He has served as Chief Executive Officer and Chairman of the Board of Directors since April 1996. He received a B.A. in Political Science from the University of Mississippi, a Masters in Organizational Management from the University of Phoenix, and the Distinguished Certified Franchise Executive Designation from the International Franchise Association for his work and study in the Franchise industry. He has received his Personal Training certification through AFAA and Suspension Training certification through TRX among other fitness training certifications. His background as an athlete includes college football and Arena Football as well as numerous bodybuilding titles including NPC National Collegiate Champion.

Mr. Smith has an extensive business background, which includes being an entrepreneur since 1986. He opened and operated Bodyplex Fitness Center from 1986 through 1989, Bay Street Tanning Boutique from 1988 through 1989, and was a licensee of three Gold's Gym locations from 1989 through 1995. Mr. Smith also opened the original Planet Beach location in New Orleans, Louisiana in 1995, and he still owns this store today. In 1996, Mr. Smith founded Planet Beach Franchising Corporation and began franchising that same year. In

2014, Mr. Smith invented a new infrared fitness sauna which is now patented. It was designed for three people to work out with virtual instruction. He opened the original HOTWORX® 24 Hour Infrared Fitness Studio in 2017 and founded the HOTWORX® Franchise in that same year.

Stephen P. Smith, founder of HOTWORX®, calls it 3D Training. You'll call it a new way to workout with the benefits of heat and infrared energy, and one of the best things that ever happened to your fitness program

Hot Exercise will show you how to obtain multiple streams of physical and mental benefits from one training method. It will arm you with the knowledge and motivation to access your inner warrior and strengthen your mind and body with more workout in less time. So if you are a beginner or if you are a professional athlete, *Hot Exercise* is your guidebook to blaze a trail through the bold new infrared fitness frontier.

A Franchise is a Team

I HAVE BEEN INVOLVED in franchising and licensing now since 1989 which is more than three decades, WOW. Time flies by.

In the late '80's and early '90's I was a licensee of three Gold's Gym locations. At that time, Gold's was "licensing" out their brand name rather than full on franchising of a system of operations. I really enjoyed being an owner of Gold's Gym locations, and still love to take trips out to the original Gold's known as the Mecca of Bodybuilding in Venice, CA. I always say that if you can't get motivated in that gym, then you just can't be motivated.

I still love that brand, but a business cannot stand on its name alone. One of the reasons that I moved on from ownership of Gold's Gym was due to their lack of system standards at that time and the lack of uniformity amongst their licensees. The brand is most important, but the biggest advantage of franchise ownership is access to a proven operating system. A great system can catapult the brand to stratospheric levels.

After three decades of franchising, I can tell you that a franchise system MUST be viewed as a team. Teamwork is the only way that a franchise can thrive and succeed in the marketplace. Franchising is a difficult business model when compared to all company owned organizations such as Starbucks where each location is fully controlled by the corporate headquarters and can mandate uniformity from the top down with compliance held in place by employees who want to keep their employment. Franchising is more difficult because it relies on expansion through a federation of independent business owners connected together by a document know as the franchise agreement. Uniformity of the brand depends on adherence to that document and can at times be testy when brand standards are not met. The best way to keep the uniformity in a franchise organization is to view it as a team effort.

General Patton said "an army is a team." A franchise is a team too!

When you view franchising as a team the entire organization makes perfect sense. The way I look at it is with the franchisor as the coaching staff and each franchise location as a player on the team. For HOTWORX and our sister brand Planet Beach it works very well as viewed in that paradigm. A paradigm is not just how you look at something, though, it is also how you think about something. With the franchising model, it must be viewed as a team but always thought of as a team too. Franchising flourishes when understood truly as a team with coaches and players striving to outperform each other and to surpass competitors from other brands.

With our corporate structure, the department responsible for support of the franchise locations is the Franchise Performance Department. The VP of that department is considered the "Head Coach" who supervises a staff of business coaches each responsible for training and motivating a group of 50 franchise locations that are each considered a "player" on their team. The performance score of each location "player" is their level of profitability.

Franchising is a team sport!

Fitness and athletics go well together, and for a fitness franchise like HOTWORX, "teamthink" resonates. Teamthink is always more powerful than an individual thinking alone. A great idea from one person has no power until it is manifested through action with a group of people. They say great minds think alike, and when multitudes of great minds begin to think and act for a team to build a special brand for everyone, magic begins to happen. The result is something extraordinary for the franchisor, the franchisee, and ultimately for the customer.

To inquire about franchising, or to learn more about the organization, please visit HOTWORX.net.